LANDMARK COLLECTOR'S LIBRARY

PAST TIMES
OF
MACCLESFIELD
VOLUME I

Dorothy Bentley Smith

Published by

Landmark Publishing Ltd
Ashbourne Hall, Cokayne Ave, Ashbourne, Derbyshire DE6 1EJ England
Tel: (01335) 347349 Fax: (01335) 347303
e-mail: landmark@clara.net
website: www.landmarkpublishing.co.uk

ISBN 1 84306 167 8

© **Dorothy Bentley Smith 2004**

Print: Cromwell Press Ltd, Trowbridge
Design: Mark Titterton
Cover: James Allsopp

Front cover top left: Chestergate early 20th century; **Top right:** the view up medieval
Wallgate before demolition of the remains of John of Macclesfield's mansion in 1933;
Bottom left: the Dormel Singers – Hazel Grove 1949 with the Worsley Harrop Memorial Cup;
Bottom right: The former C. of E. chapel in the public cemetery, Prestbury Road.

Title page and back cover: Winter in Macclesfield looking across Bollin Valley
to the Silk Road and St. Paul's C. of E.

LANDMARK COLLECTOR'S LIBRARY

PAST TIMES
OF
MACCLESFIELD

VOLUME I

Dorothy Bentley Smith

Landmark Publishing

Dedication

To my grand-daughters Megan Eveline and Charlotte Elizabeth
and all future generations.

*'Ignorance is the first requisite of the historian-
ignorance, which simplifies and clarifies,
which selects and omits, with a placid perfection
unattainable by the highest art.'*

Lytton Strachey (1880-1932)

Contents

INDEX AND NOTES ON REFERENCES ARE INCLUDED IN VOLUME II

Foreword

To commemorate ten years of writing for the Macclesfield Community News, and with encouragement from my publisher and others, I decided that the time was right to produce a collection of my local history articles in book form.

It is inevitable, when writing for a newspaper, that occasions will arise when editing takes place, or photographs and even articles omitted, because of limited space (for this reason no articles appeared in the September 2000 and 2001 editions). This has given me the opportunity to publish the unedited versions, correct errors where necessary and add the additional illustrations. I sincerely hope that this book will not only be of interest as a general read, but will also be used for research purposes and encourage a further generation to appreciate the wealth of history which lies within the borough of Macclesfield.

Dorothy Bentley Smith

Acknowledgements

Late in the summer of 1994 Granville Sellars, the then owner of the Macclesfield Community News, offered me the opportunity to write a series of local history articles for the free monthly newspaper. I eagerly accepted, but neither he nor I could have envisaged that ten years on I would still be contributing my column; and so to him must go my first vote of thanks.

It has been a fascinating and rewarding journey made possible, not only by the Macclesfield people of the past, but also those of the present who have helped in several ways. Many have generously given permission for property deeds to be examined; produced old books, long since removed from accessible bookshelves; donated photographs and information, and invited me into their homes.

I am also indebted to numerous solicitors; estate agents; personnel within banks, breweries, head offices of businesses investing in High Street shops; the Macclesfield Borough Council and the Silk Heritage Centre, for their co-operation. Nor must I forget the staff of the Cheshire County Record Office and Macclesfield Public Library who have been indefatigable in searching out relevant sources of information; and the Leeds District Archivist who spent time and effort in putting at my disposal a considerable volume of information from the large Radcliffe family archive (Pickford family) part of which was uncatalogued. Also to my eldest daughter, Victoria, whose skills and knowledge in the mysterious world of computers is second to none, and to the staff of Mailboxes Etc. who have given considerable assistance with illustrations over the years in reproducing specific details from photos and plans.

Last, but by no means least, my thanks must go to the excellent 'team' in the Community News offices, and in particular to the editor, Jean Ellis, whose support and encouragement over the last decade have been very much appreciated.

Maps of Macclesfield

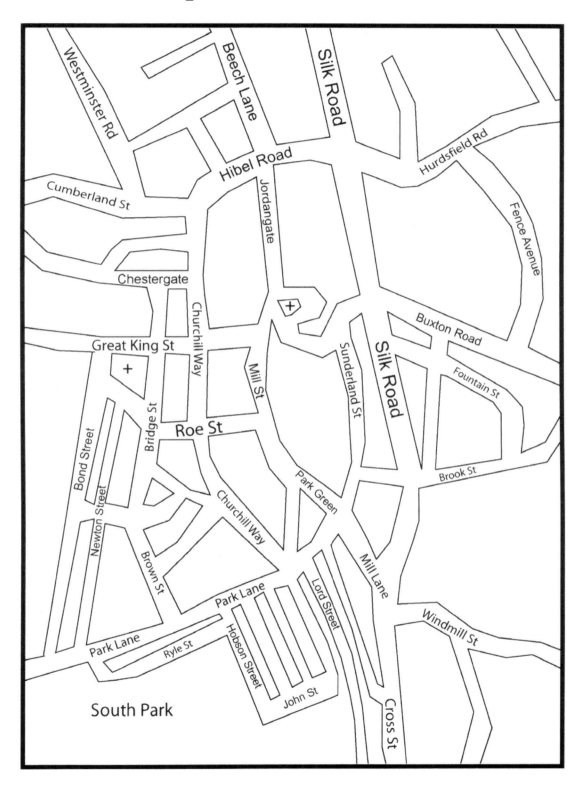

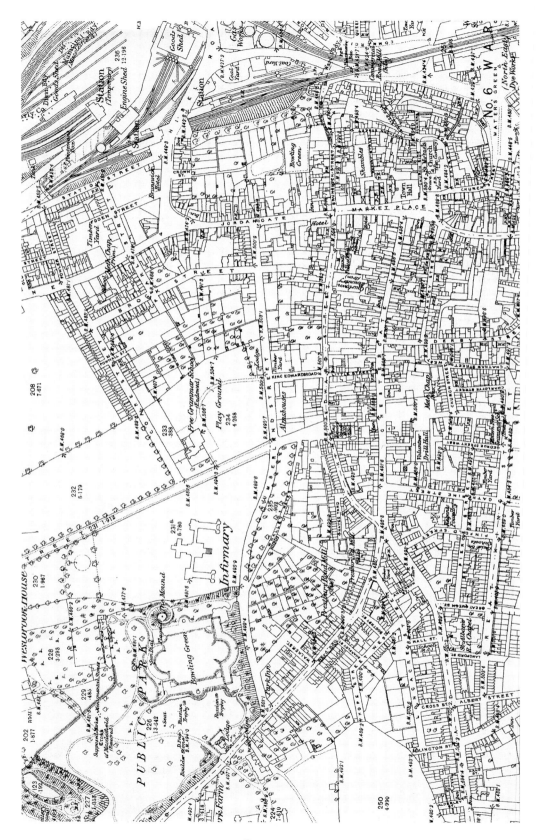

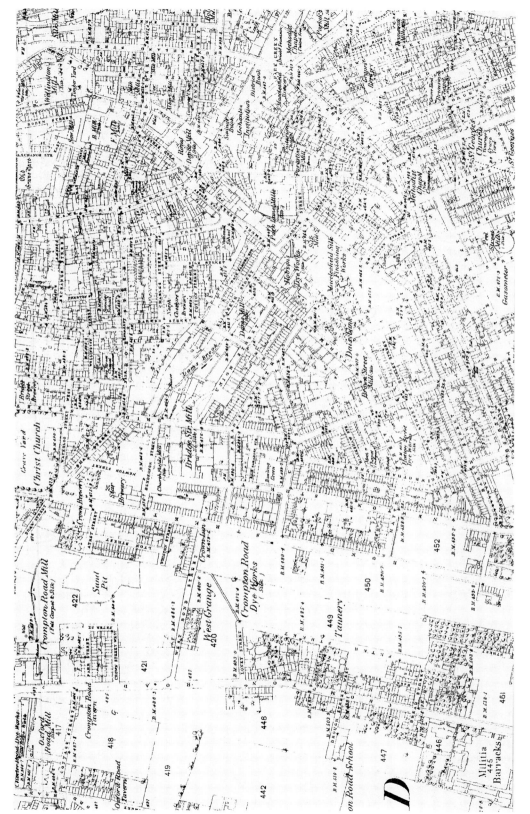

Reproduced from the 1871 Ordnance Survey Map

9

Macclesfield Town Centre

Where better to begin a series of articles on local history than in the centre of town? Yet, if asked, many people might have differing views as to where the centre of Macclesfield is. Today I think the vast majority of residents would site it as the Market Place, where St. Michael's Church stands and where the remains of the old Market Cross pose defiantly as if to remind strangers of Macclesfield's historic past.

View of the Market Place in 1994 showing the entrance to the Grosvenor centre on the left, formerly Stanley Street, and before that Dog Lane. In the centre was a possible burgage plot – privately owned by a burgess of the town. On the right was the site of the Angel Inn, a famous coaching house.

This view would certainly coincide with that of early 18th century residents who gathered in the Market Place to hear news, public announcements, proclamations and the like. To them the Cross was the important focal point of any public meeting, but sadly many locals now pass it by without even a cursory glance. Considered as a conveniently large traffic island, its 'home' was the approximate area occupied by two shops in the early 18th century. (Since writing this, the Market square has been reorganised and the Cross moved from the centre to the south-east corner).

St. Michael's is, of course, situated on the eastern side of the square, which helps locate the position of the shops. A deed of 15th September 1715 gives the estimated size of the site as, east to west 30ft. (9 metres) in length, and north to south 21ft. (6.5 metres) in breadth.

Unfortunately there is no indication of which way the shops faced, but breadth seems to indicate frontage, as on many deeds I have seen the phrase 'Breadth to the Street'. So I suggest that they were back to back, with one facing what was then the Parochial Chapel (referred to as St. Michael's after extensive rebuilding in 1740), and the other facing the then Dog Lane; a possible burgage plot and the Angel Inn (now the Mill St. Mall, Grosvenor Centre; premises adjoining the entrance in the Market Place on the northern side; and part of the NatWest Bank premises, respectively).

It is logical to assume that earlier buildings had occupied the site of the two shops. During excavations in 1878 the remains of a doorway of an ancient Guildhall, and part of the foundations, were said to have been discovered in line with the north side of the churchyard. As mouldings of a gateway or double entrance were also laid bare, it is possible that the Victorian excavators had discovered the remains from the shops, demolished in 1778, at the start of what was to be extensive alterations to the Market Place, taking several years to complete.

In September 1715 Thomas Motterhead of Tytherington became the owner and leased these shops to tenants. His ownership was only possible because he had negotiated a loan with a joiner, Philemon Mainwaring and wife, Ruth. Until the late 18th century quite often builders appeared under the guise of bricklayers, 'joyners' (joiners) or 'plaisterers' (plasterers), so the information on the deeds suggests that Philemon Mainwaring had built the shops and then, in order to sell them, had created a mortgage for a would-be purchaser. It was very difficult at that period to obtain loans, the Bank of England was newly established (in 1694) and experimentation of branch banking was only tentatively underway in Scotland, but even that did not last long.

Thomas Mottershead came from a numerous family, many of whom lived in the vicinity of Alderley Edge and Mottram Andrew (N.B. no Saint!). One is said to have collected rents on behalf of the Parliamentarian officer, Sir William Brereton of Handforth. Thomas was a favourite family Christian name making attribution difficult at times, but if not the same person, certainly a kinsman of the same name made a fortune in London during the Commonwealth period as a dungster. This presumably gave him responsibility for the collection and disposal of human and animal excrement by scavengers, and its conversion into manure – an extremely important commodity sometimes mentioned in property deeds, to ensure it was left for use by the next occupier when land was vacated.

With his fortune Thomas purchased several properties in Chester on Foregate Street and Fleshmongers Lane. The deed of 6th June 1662, two years after the Restoration, shows the vendor as Peter Warburton of Arley Hall, Cheshire. Perhaps Thomas had organised supplies of manure for the original gardens, the precursors of those which give so much pleasure and enjoyment to visitors today.

Returning to the Market Place in Macclesfield, if the two shops covered the present site of the Market Cross, where did the Cross originally stand? A clue can be found in a letter relating to the early 1730s. During an Election campaign (which were always lively affairs) a large concourse of townspeople had gathered in the Market Place 'near to the Angel and were making merry' when one of the campaigners, who was standing at the door of the Inn 'facing the people in the Market Place sent out a Barrel of Ale to be drank at the Cross' . . . This suggests that the Cross was not too far distant, and probably close to the Angel Inn. The Angel was, of course, demolished in the early 1970s to make way for the NatWest Bank extension; but that's another story.

The Cross was removed in 1795 as part of the reorganisation plan of the area. Discarded at a time when Macclesfield was loosening its ancient shackles and looking forward to a modern 19th century, it now deserves recognition for its deeper symbolic significances.

Carved into one of the foot-stones is the inscription 'M.W.W. 1798' which obviously has no direct connection with the Cross as it originally stood near to the Angel Inn, but it appears to have an indirect connection which will be discussed later in the series.

The year 1798 neatly draws to a close the 18th century. With William and Mary's encouragement of a Bank of England, what had begun in 1694 as a period of incredible versatility, wealth and sheer genius, ended in 1797 with the importation of grain on a permanent basis. A nation with a population explosion, no longer able to feed itself, and a military genius in the

The remains of the old Market Cross removed to this site in 1971.

11

form of Napoleon Bonaparte ready to take advantage of every opportunity to seize power in Europe, was a perfect recipe for disaster. Small wonder the Cross was forgotten in the traumatic period which followed. After sixty years and various misfortunes, what remained was given a temporary resting place in West Park, until its final limited reconstruction in the Market Place during 1971.

* * *

For most of the 18th century the Macclesfield Market Place remained almost a third of the size it is today. Bound on the east by two shops, which effectively blocked out the panoramic view of the Parochial Chapel in the foreground, extending to the Gritstone Ridge below Tegg's Nose in the distance, the area was more compact and intimate, thus more appropriate to the 'Vill' (town) of Macclesfield at that period.

Light post coach 1817.

On the left is the Angel Hotel circa 1940. Photos taken earlier in the century show an elaborate wrought iron balustrade above the ground floor facade complete with exterior gas light. These must have been removed as part of the World War II effort, fortunately revealing the Inn as it appeared when Samuel Goodwin was landlord in the last quarter of the 18th century.

Accommodation was vital when carrying valuable merchandise, and it was also important to carry letters of introduction if not known in a particular place. A merchant of importance would often accommodate another of similar standing, being a friend or associate; and the servant of the visiting merchant would be welcomed in his servant's quarters. Obviously there were occasions, particularly as the century progressed and more and more travellers took to the road, when hostelries were used. So the old taverns, many of which had existed for centuries, began to modernise and develop into grand coaching stations, in the hope of providing more 'appropriate' facilities for their guests; the Angel Inn of Macclesfield was one of them.

The Angel occupied an important site in the Market Place, which suggests that there would have been an inn there from at least the medieval period. Although early deeds are missing, the site has erroneously been ascribed to part of a plot containing the townhouse of the Stanley family. Certainly it would have covered at least one or two burgages, but although burgage plots were previously owned by the Mayor, Aldermen and Burgesses as a Corporate body, by the 18th century many were privately owned and subleased as a form of investment.

By the early 18th century London could boast of six Angel inns. In all probability the one in Macclesfield was named after its famous counterpart in the Clerkenwell parish (often mistakenly sited in Islington and remembered today by the Angel Underground station). This London inn, first recorded in 1611 when the Company of Merchant Taylors held a dinner there, became a famous resting place on the Great North Road for travellers to and from the City.

Victorian railway stations would later adopt the same names as their London counterparts, but it would seem that the process had already been well established by their fore-runners, the coaching inns. Not only did Macclesfield's premier hostelry become the Angel, but also one in Dale St. for Liverpool.

The Macclesfield inn was well patronised by the 1730s, suggesting a 17th century origin. Rooms were hired by visiting chapmen for the sale of goods e.g. in 1738 a Samuel Reddish, who travelled by Licence from town to town and dealt in upholstered goods (this included carpets), 'opened a room' in the Angel and 'dispersed printed Bills up and down the Town to give Notice of his Sale thereof by Wholsesale or Retail'. He appears to have visited once a year, as did a travelling Jew.

The 1760s saw the development of balls and assemblies, so reminiscent of 'The Crown Inn' as described in Jane Austen's novel, 'Emma'.

Throughout the centuries the Angel played host to many groups of people attending property sales and auctions, which were advertised in the Chester, Manchester and Derby newspapers; as yet Macclesfield had no newspaper of its own.

There were even adverts for the auctioning of mining shares, as evidenced by an insert in the *Derby Mercury* of 15th July 1768, headed 'At the house of Mr. William Hilton being the Sign of the Angel in Macclesfield'. An advert of 20th Oct. 1772 refers to a sale 'at the Sign of the New Angel in Macclesfield' suggesting modernised premises. (The façade in the photo must relate to the 'New Angel').

About that time four new buildings were added at the rear causing a dispute some 20 years later (1795) when the then landlord, Samuel Goodwin, decided to make a window in each of them i.e. 'the Back Parlour; 'the Brewhouse; ' the Grainery' and' the Laundery'. Charles Simpson, landlord of the Sun Inn, Chestergate, objected, commenting that his yard was now 'overlooked which is very disagreeable', and immediately constructed a partition to cover up the offending panes!

Samuel Goodwin accepted that he was at fault but begged the favour of retaining the 'Lights' (windows) whilst he and his family remained in occupation. Because of 'the Friendship that have for several Years subsisted' Charles Simpson agreed and accepted 'a Bottle of Wine Yearly for (allowing) such Privilege' . . .

A Victorian O.S. map (1871) confirms the existence of a passageway leading from the Market Place, along the southern side of the building, into a rear yard. Obviously stabling facilities would be provided.

The Old Angel, in 1745, had been regarded as the best of several good inns in the town 'for good entertainment and civil usage'. It seems apparent that Samuel Goodwin now had grand designs to establish the inn as an elite coaching station, though whether or not he succeeded can be judged from the following accounts.

On Sunday, 14th September 1777, James Boswell, intent on visiting his great friend Dr.

Johnson in Ashbourne, took the coach from Manchester. 'At Macclesfield I did not find the Inn to my mind. So I drove to Leek . . . slept pretty well'. One must ask whether or not it was the Inn he objected to or the maids, for on awakening in Leek he records that he 'fondled' the chambermaid!

The Torrington Diaries, written by the Hon. John Byng, who was not the best person in the world to please, record three of his visits, the first during 1784:

'In this inn are built assembly and tea rooms of spacious grandeur where are held monthly assemblies, at which the maid brag'd that none but gentility were admitted: but on no account any tradesmen' . . .

A brief visit of 1790 found him 'happy to attack a boild Buttock of A Bull'.

Two years later he wrote 'I put up at the best, tho' a bad inn (where I have been before). The Angel, where the house was so crouded by a grand dinner – that I betook myself into a small room behind the bar'. The dinner was for the Sick & Burial Society members, founded by the 'old women of the town'. He enjoyed the dinner, 'a good ham', but was 'properly peeved next day when, having walked to the Roe & Co. copper works on Macclesfield Common, he was refused entry without a ticket, and was forced 'to trudge a mile back' to the company banking house to obtain one. (The bank was situated only two minutes from the Angel).

In spite of all, Samuel Goodwin was elected Mayor for the year 1801-2.

With the building of a superior hotel – The Macclesfield Arms – early in the 19th century, the Angel appears to have given up all sales and auctions: however, the 1825 *Macclesfield Directory* records John Hodginson as landlord of the inn and 'Posting House, Market Place. This was a prestigious franchise, bringing with it considerable revenue. A far cry from the day in 1704 when John Ward, lawyer of Capesthorne Hall, had written that Macclesfield was not accepting post for Manchester, instead of which it was being directed through Knutsford, so 'there's an end of all hopes of making Macclesfield a post town'.

Remarkably, throughout at least 300 years of existence, the Angel never changed its name. Demolished in 1971 to make way for an extension of the NatWest Bank premises, it is now remembered within the bank by a photo hanging on a wall.

St. Michael's Parish Church

CHRISTMAS – 'a feftival of the Christian church, observed on the 25th December. in memory of the nativity of Jefus Christ' – a definition according to the original Encyclopaedia Britannica published in Edinburgh 1771. (note the use of f instead of s in some words; a tradition still in use in 1771 from handwritten manuscripts. The letter was known as a descending s but began to disappear from print circa 1785).

The reason this date was chosen is uncertain, but general belief suggests that it was the Christian alternative to a pagan festival of agriculture and solar observances. Roman Christians were already observing Christmas by A.D. 336; the Eastern Empire, however, continued to commemorate 'the Manifestation of God in both the birth and baptism of Jesus' on the 6th January, but gradually accepted the Western date. One exception remained: the Armenian Church, which still today observes the 6th January.

Fires and lights, symbols of warmth and lasting life, have always been associated with both the pagan and Christian festivals, which, together with customs assimilated from other cultures, have contributed towards our present day festivities.

Since the Middle Ages evergreens have symbolised survival. German and Celtic Yule rites

Above left: Celebrating Christmas at the Parish Church of St. Michael and All Angels. **Above right:** One of a matching pair of superb brass candelabra in the Parish Church. Originally cast by William Alexander & Co., Woodstreet, London, with a flame finial and two tiers, it probably held 20 large candles. William Alexander was described as a fine worker in brass at London Wall on admission to the Tallow Chandlers' Co in 1716. He was elected Master of the Company in 1747. This is another indication of Macclesfield's strong commercial links with London at that time. This candelabrum appears to have been recast to match the one given by Mary Hooley who died 26th July 1822. Its remodelled dove finial is an appropriate reminder of the Christmas message 'Peace on Earth, Goodwill towards Men".

have ensured plenty of food and good fellow-ship, but the Christmas card is of relatively late inclusion. Designed in England 1843, a limited edition of 1,000 copies was sold in London. The card depicted a jolly family party beneath which was written 'A Merry Christmas and a Happy New Year to you'.

Elizabethan England celebrated Christmas as a solely religious festival, although the Court did present gifts to the Queen at New Year. The great enthusiast who did much to encourage our ideas of a truly Victorian 'English' Christmas was, of course, the Consort of Queen Victoria, Prince Albert; so where does this place the 18th century Georgians with regard to their festivities?

Firstly, it is extremely difficult to find many references to Christmas in diaries, journals, day-books or even novels of the period. The 25th December was regarded as a Sunday and everyone as far as possible went to church. The occasional mention suggests a time for visiting friends and taking presents of food, or providing for the poor.

A vicar's niece in Norfolk wrote in her diary for Tuesday, 25th December 1792 'Uncle had six poor old Men to Dinner in the Kitchen, gave them for Dinner Roast Beef and Plum Pudding, small Beer and Strong and to each a Shilling a Piece to carry home to their wives'. Another diary, kept by an acquaintance of the Roe family of Macclesfield briefly mentions that on 24th Dec. 1774 he dined with friends and gave them a 'Side of Venison'. He also dines out on the 28th and 31st taking with him on both occasions 'some fresh Cod'.

Surprisingly, apart from being Christmas Day, the 25th December, known as a Quarter Day, marked the end of an accounting period. In fact there still remains on Park Lane a group of properties having Ground Rents payable each 25th December. An extract from a Steward's letter dated 9th February 1784 shows what a busy period it could be, 'Your Lordship's Acc(oun)ts. now take up a great deal of Time. My son has not spent a day in any other Businefs since the 25th of Decemr. and it has occupied three fourths of my Time during the same period'.

Quarter Days reflected the strong hold the Church had on everyday life. A will proved in 1765 clearly stipulates that, what was in effect a pension to the widow, had to be made in equal quarterly payments at the usual Feast or days of payment of rent in the year (that is to say Michaelmas, Christmas, Lady Day and Midsummer).

Midsummer Day (24th June) was not very popular as a payment day because people tended to make demands half-yearly at Michaelmas (29th September) and Lady Day (25th March); again reflecting dates on which many Ground Rents are still payable. Unusually the Cholmondeley Estate originally charged rents for Macclesfield Park at Midsummer and Martinmas (11th November) although the latter is a Quarter Day in Scotland.

Lady Day was regarded by the Church of England as the first day of the new year, that is until 1752 when a traumatic change took place.

In order to align ourselves with most European countries, New Year's Day became 1st. January, but the calendar was also corrected according to astronomical calculations, and 11 days were removed. For that year only the day after the 2nd September became the 14th instead of the 3rd., much to the chagrin of many Englishmen who considered they had been cheated! Perhaps some were with regard to rents payable, although in many instances adjustments were made. An odd reference in some mining accounts states that the figures used would be up to 'The Old Christmas Day' not the 'New', which by then would, of course, be the 6th January.

The Treasury moved its year end forward 11 days from Lady Day (actually taken up to the previous day i.e. 24th March), to compensate, so that to this day the 5th April is one of the best known dates in our calendar. Even the Cholmondeley Estate followed suit and the rentals for Macclesfield Park became due up to the 5th April.

* * *

Under a new charter granted by Elizabeth I in 1595, a yearly election was granted to the Capital Burgesses on the Friday after Michaelmas, by which they chose one of their number as mayor. The mayors of the 18th century and earlier were personally responsible for the Corporation accounts, so the retiring mayor each year could make them up to the Quarter Day of Michaelmas.

One mayor of Macclesfield. who unfortunately did not quite live long enough to complete either his term of office or his accounts was Thomas Hooley. He died in September

1744 but left money in his will for 'the purchase of a Candle Stick for the Use of the Parochiall Chappel of Macclesfield'. The magnificent candelabrum, partially recast in 1822 to match its new partner, symbolises so well the Christmas spirit of warmth and everlasting life.

By his will of 1744 Thomas Hooley, Mayor of Macclesfield, not only left his money for the purchase of the superb brass candelabrum, which still hangs in the Parish Church but also left £10 (at least £1,000 today) 'to be laid out in the purchase of a Marble Font of Derbyshire Marble. . .'

This font is unique, being the only one in Cheshire, and possibly the only one in England, to have its own polished wooden plinth with wheels. It must have travelled many miles during its existence, because it is easily and frequently moved around the church for the convenience of christenings.

In the 18th century, especially the latter half, the use of marble by the aristocracy was considerable, as more and more ancestral homes were rebuilt or extended and refurbished. Soon the middle classes followed suit and wealthy merchants, tradesmen, lawyers, apothecaries, officers in the militia, soapmakers and even butchers, bakers and candlestick makers were making enough money to copy their wealthy neighbours or landlords.

The most expensive and desirable marble came from the town of Carrara, just to the northwest of Leghorn in Northern Italy. It was a white statuary marble described as 'very fine' and more 'compact'. Many pale yellow glossy marbles were found throughout Italy but a variety of coloured ones were also available, either found naturally or 'dyed'.

Dyeing was an extremely difficult process in which the marble had to be heated to a temperature, not too low nor too high, to enable it to receive the colours. A variety of ingredients could be used including green wax (green), pitch and turpentine (brown) and fine powdered cochineal well dissolved in urine and quicklime (vermillion). In order to fix the colours different concoctions were used as appropriate. Many responded well to 'spirit of wine' but a popular one was 'horse's or dog's urine with four parts quicklime and one part pot-ashes.'

No such colouring was necessary to promulgate the beauty of Thomas Hooley's font, only

The coat of arms legitimately used by Thomas Percival of Royton Hall near Oldham. Thomas, a famous antiquarian, gave the land upon which Royton Church was built in 1754 and held coal mining rights on Macclesfield Common.
The coat of arms: the left half with its horse passant relates to the Percival family; the right half with its three trefoils relates to the family of his wife, Martha, the Greggs of Chamber Hall, Oldham.
Their only child, Katherine, married Joseph Pickford after whom Pickford Street in Macclesfield is named.

The font of Derbyshire marble in the Parish Church.

the expert hands of a master mason. The pale coloured pinkish or 'whiteish brown commonly called Darby-marble' was ideal for sculpturing, causing no distraction due to vivid colours. The marble was quarried in the immediate area of Monyash, where also occurred a pale grey or black mottled variety, sometimes containing beautiful veins of deep purple. Although 'Derby marble' seems to have been used as a generic term, yet there is little doubt that the Hooley font was from Derbyshire.

Because of an extremely rare black marble localised to an area near Ashford (now suffixed 'in the Water') a thriving marble works was established there in 1748 and, as a result of typical Georgian curiosity, gained favour as a tourist attraction. A visitor's description of 1765 shows how difficult the operations for preparing marble could be.

Blocks of marble 'from 3 to 4 or 4½ (?ft) long' were fixed under steel plates 'drawn Tite (tight) by screws and wedges' but could be moved backwards and forwards by means of cranks. Stone saws were used for cutting and the visitor noted 'Eight inches a day is deemed a day's work.' During the process the marble slabs were covered with coarse sand on to which water was continually dripped.

Having been reduced to convenient sizes (the black marble was very desirable for chimney pieces etc) they were then taken to a mill, where, by means of a revolving wheel, the blocks passed through a 'sludge of Chaft Sand and Water about the consistence of Tar or Treacle.' This removed the saw marks after which they were taken to the 'Polishing Mill' where pumice stone and emery (a dull bluish-black mineral used in polishing glass) made them acceptable for fashioning by the masons.

The expertise for this work must already have been available in the area before the establishment of the marble works.

Charles Roe's brother-in-law, who was a very important mining manager, had his home in Ashford but was buried in Monyash some months later. It seems more than likely that Charles would have had a hand in commissioning the font; both he and Thomas Hooley served together as members of the Corporation.

*　*　*

Whilst the advent of the Roes to Macclesfield was of fairly recent date, the Hooleys had long been established in the town and Thomas was living in the Wall House on Back Street (King Edward Street) at the time of his death.

The original family name was Howley adapted to Hooley by the 18th century, but great confusion has arisen with the Hulley family because two Hooley sisters married two Hulley brothers. They could have originated from a common ancestor for both had strong connections with East Lancashire, indicative of an association with the 'cotton wool' trade which was, in reality, wool. This later developed into the cotton industry as we know it today, with the importation of raw cotton from the colonies.

The earliest mention in the first Parish register is of a Lawrence Hooley (Howley) marrying Ales Parcyvall at Prestbury on 2nd July 1592. Alice, baptised in the Collegiate Church, Christ's Church (now Manchester Cathedral) was the daughter of Thomas Parcyvall (Percival) and this is how the name was introduced into the Hooley family; Lawrence and Alice baptised their son, Thomas, in St Michael's chapel, Macclesfield during 1595.

The Hulleys do not appear in Macclesfield before the 18th century, but are remembered today by Hulley Road in Hurdsfield because of their land holdings in that area.

Thomas Hooley is still remembered by Hooley Range in Heaton Norris where he owned Spout House, an estate with several lands etc. which he willed to his brother, John, of Macclesfield. His sister, Rebecca, received 'One seat in the New Square pew' incorporated into St Michael's during the extensive alterations of 1740.

Amongst the Percival kinsmen, Thomas of Royton Hall near Oldham held rights to the coal mines on Macclesfield Common in the 1740s, but it was an ancestor, Sir John, who should be best remembered as the Founder of the Free Grammar School (The King's School, Macclesfield) in 1503.

*　*　*

At the time of the Domesday survey, Macclesfield belonged to the Earls of Chester but soon passed into the Royal possession, and its unique history has evolved from the fact that it became part of the Marriage Settlements of two Queens of England.

Eleanor, first wife of Edward I (1270-90) has always been credited with founding the chapel on the present site of St. Michael's Church. Her

The Savage Tower, behind which lies the family chapel built 1504-7. Founder: Thomas Savage who, as Archbishop of York, was buried in York Minster in 1507. The three storeyed tower was the original 'house' of the priest, who was also teacher of the Grammar School. The crenellated top has been rebuilt and the heraldry above the door, carefully preserved.

personal interest was passed to Isabella, wife of Edward II, who became involved in her husband's brutal murder.

These two Royal ladies granted such extensive privileges to the Manor (Edward I had already granted a charter in 1261, making Macclesfield a free Borough with a Merchant Guild) that finally there was doubt whether or not it had ever been part of Cheshire. Even County officials were excluded from interfering in Macclesfield's local government, a privilege which was still being jealously guarded by the Mayor, Aldermen and Burgesses of the early 18th century.

Unfortunately, the situation gave rise to mismanagement by one or two local officials and the Manor became 'decayed and demoralised'.

In 1347, Queen Isabella was persuaded by her grandson, the Black Prince, to exchange Macclesfield for two of his manors in Wiltshire and Dorset, so the re-integration of Macclesfield into Cheshire began.

Sir Thomas Ferrers, Chief Justice (justiciar) of Chester was made steward and bailiff of the Manor and Hundred from March 16th 1348, but in 1349, the Black Death arrived. It has been reckoned that about half the Macclesfield population perished during the ravages of the plague, which made rents difficult to collect and left large strips of land untenanted.

In 1353, the Black Prince visited Macclesfield and generously put to right the wrongs of his over zealous revenue collector – a colourful character named Adam Mottram – who had been given the job by Thomas Ferrers in the autumn of 1347. Adam Mottram was also hereditary gaoler and very adept at collecting heriots (a right of a landlord under copyhold tenure to the best live beast or property on a tenant's death. Often a piece of silver was 'seized'. Surprisingly, this was not abolished until 1935). He was eventually pardoned for his misdemeanours after taking part in the Black Prince's military campaign to Gascony, an ancient province in south west France, near the Pyrenees, which was held under the English crown from 1360 to 1451.

At his death, Mottram was quite a wealthy man and willed his investments to his son, John, but, as often happens, a powerful father produces a weaker son, and early in the 15th century, the former holdings of Mottram were mortgaged to John Savage. This is the first mention in Macclesfield of the Savage family of Stainsby in Derbyshire. Their military, trading and aristocratic connections helped to foster their increase in power and wealth.

Sir John Savage, politician and soldier, who died in 1492, was selected as a bearer to carry Edward IV's body into Westminster Abbey, and it is his parents whose effigies lie to the right of the high altar in St. Michael's and provide excellent detail of the costumes of the period, particularly the lady's headdress.

* * *

Sir John's brother eventually became Archbishop of York and was responsible for building the Savage Chapel and Tower, adjacent to, but now part of the main body of the church. The family mansion of Rock Savage, near Runcorn, was built by yet another Sir John in 1565, but the family retained their valuable land holdings in Macclesfield, the greater part of which was Macclesfield Park.

Today, Park Lane and its continuation, Ivy Lane, conveniently provide a line which cuts the old parkland almost into two equal parts. The boundary ran along what is now Roe Street in a line westwards to the Chester Road roundabout. It continued up Chester Road and turned to follow approximately Ivy Road crossing Ullswater, towards the Rising Sun Public House on Gawsworth Road. But at some point, it turned once more so that the southern boundary followed the general direction of Moss Lane to Parkgate Road. The eastern boundary ran in a northerly line to Park Green, then up Mill Street to rejoin Roe Street. The remnant still remaining is, of course, South Park which, as its name implies, was in the southern half of the parkland.

In 1639, the then Viscount Savage inherited the earldom of Rivers and Viscounty of Colchester in Essex under a special grant from his wife's father. He was High Steward of Macclesfield and a Colonel in the Royal Army who fought alongside Prince Rupert at Bristol during the Civil War. He was later buried in Macclesfield, having been 'late a prisoner in the upper branch prison in Southwark Co. Surrey'.

His son, Thomas, who was very proud of his titles, styling himself 'Viscount Rocksavage' is commemorated by a magnificent monument. He also was High Steward of Macclesfield and buried within the church, but Thomas's son, Richard, left a very different kind of monument.

Swift wrote: 'He has left legacies to about twenty paltry whores by name and not a farthing to any friend, dependent or relation' (except his second cousin, a Roman Catholic priest whom he treated 'like a footman')... 'I love the man, but detest his memory'.

The parkland must have been part of the Marriage Settlement of his daughter because it passed eventually to his granddaughter, wife of General James Cholmondeley. As the couple had no children, the Savage involvement in Macclesfield came to an end after more than 300 years.

General Cholmondeley, buried in Westminster Abbey on 19th October 1775, left the land and premises to his nephew, George, Earl of Cholmondeley, who immediately had a survey carried out.

The lands appear to have been mortgaged, probably because of financial difficulties, and an Act of 1787 confirmed ownership to Earl Cholmondeley, resulting in a grand sale of virtually all his Macclesfield possessions during the spring of 1788. The one notable exception entered on all property deeds was 'the Chapel called Earl River's Chapel adjoining the Parochial Chapel of Macclesfield . . . and the Cemetary (sic) or Burial Ground under the same' which was to remain in possession of the Earls of Cholmondeley.

The magnificent monument of Thomas, 3rd Earl Rivers and Viscount Colchester, who died in 1694. His pride of titles will never be forgotten – his eulogy says it all! It is considered to be one of the finest works of the famous Stuart sculptor, William Stanton, by whom it is signed

Grammar School
(now The King's School)

One thing which never fails to surprise is how quickly the location of a well-known or important site, building or monument etc. is soon forgotten – particularly after the destruction of its fabric. The city of Troy has proved a debating point for decades and, on a smaller scale, Macclesfield has not been without its own controversies.

Arguments and speculation regarding the original site of the Free Grammar School (now King's School) have surfaced from time to time, but at last it has been possible to untangle its early history.

When Henry Tudor, born at Pembroke Castle in Wales, defeated Richard III on Bosworth Field in 1485 to claim the English throne as Henry VII, he brought to an end the Wars of the Roses by marrying Elizabeth of York, daughter of Edward IV.

This had not been such a dramatic period as is often presented; fighting was restricted to small areas with few people involved. Towns were not attacked and it was, in reality, family feuding.

Henry crossed the Welsh border carrying Cadwallader's red dragon on his banner and not only founded the Tudor dynasty, but took an England of considerable wealth, due mainly to the woollen cloth trade.

Surprisingly after the Black Death plague in the mid-14th century economic recovery had been rapid, as a great demand for British wool arose due to its superior quality. By the reign of Henry VII the raw wool exports had steadily decreased, but the art of weaving had been mastered so well that woollen cloth became dominant in the export market.

Even in the early 18th century a wool-stapler was described as a tradesman 'who is the Sheet Anchor of Great Britain'. The wool was brought from farms in the country and kept in large warehouses in London. It was also sorted for the manufacturers, although again cloth was woven in the country, with much being brought to the London market for sale.

The original cloth market had been at

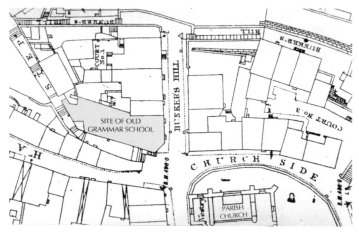

Part of the 1871 O.S. map on which I have shown the site of the Old Grammar School in relation to the Parish Church of St.Michael's.

Smithfield, but in 1123 the Priory of St. Bartholomew the Great was built on the site. In order to provide money for the upkeep of the church, Henry I agreed to the establishment of a three-day fair on the feast of St. Bartholomew (24th August) each year. This became the market for clothiers and drapers, attracting merchants from as far away as Flanders and Italy.

Soon the powerful Guild of the Merchant Taylors' Company sent members, each carrying a silver yard measure, to check the yardsticks of the vendors in the market and prevent short measures being sold.

During the year in which Henry VII became King, John Percyvale (Percival), almost 50 years of age, was elected Master of the Merchant Tailors' Company and became Sheriff the following year (1486). His family appear to have been from the Manchester area, with relatives in Stockport, although in his own words he was born 'fast' by Macclesfield. This does not necessarily mean very close by, but is indicative of his family's involvement in Macclesfield and the wool trade.

John was considered important enough to be

View from behind St Michael's Church looking towards Kerridge Hill. To the left of the picture in the foreground is the site of the Macclesfield Grammar School from c.1553 to 1748. Only a small part of the building would have been within the boundary of Sparrow Park today.

funds needed to build his Savage tower and chapel, and he must have agreed to engage a kinsman of Sir John, William Bridges, to be first 'maister' of the school.

The Bridges family were from Stockport, where a grammar school had already been founded in 1488 by another former Lord Mayor of London, Edmund Shaa (Shaw) a goldsmith, formerly of Dukinfield. The provisions made for the Macclesfield school were almost identical to those of Stockport ie. a priest to chant Mass daily for the soul of the founder etc. with school governors appointed.

Sir John died in 1503 and work began on the Savage Chapel the following year, at which time William Bridges took up his duties of priest and schoolmaster, a post he would hold for more than 30 years until his death. There seems little doubt that the small school was held in his house built as part of the Savage tower and chapel.

By his will dated 10th March 1536 William Bridges requested to be buried near the choir side of the altar to St. James in the church of 'All Hallowes' (now St. Michael's). If possible he wished for 30 priests to sing and say prayers during the night of his funeral, for which each would receive 8 pence. For those of the thirty who were vicars or parish priests, the generous payment of 12 pence was to be made. Nor did he forget his pupils at the 'Grammar Schole': those who could sing were to have 2 pence and the others one penny.

Henry VIII in his efforts to rid England of the large payments demanded from wealthy monasteries by the Pope in Rome, seized all Church properties and transferred them to the State during the years 1536-40. This was unfortunate for the Macclesfield Grammar School as there was no additional income for a new master. However, during the reign of Henry's young son, Edward VI a petition from some of the surviving governors 'for a Grammar School to be erected and established in Macclesfield . . . for the institution and instruction of children and youth in Grammar' was successful. The school, re-founded on 25th April 1552, was to have one 'Master or Tutor' and one 'Sub-tutor or Usher'.

one of the guests at a feast given for young Prince Henry (later Henry VIII) on the 11th November 1494, who, although only three years old, had been made Lieutenant of Ireland and then Duke of York.

As Alderman Percyvale he was called to arms by the City's Lord Mayor in 1497 to defend the Crown for Henry VII against rebels gathered south of the River Thames at Blackheath near Greenwich (scene of the Peasants' Revolt in 1381, after which the then Lord Mayor of London had successfully quelled the rebellion by slaying Wat Tyler at Smithfield). This was the Alderman's finest hour – after the rebels' defeat Henry VII knighted him on the battlefield, and within the year he was Lord Mayor of the City of London.

Sir John was the first of the Merchant Tailors' Company to hold this prestigious office and the Company paid the expenses for his inaugural procession. It must have been a grand affair; a trumpet with eight banners was purchased, together with a sword 'whereof the Crosse and pomell is plated with silver & overgilt'.

Late in life, having married the widow of another Guild member and being without children, Sir John was persuaded by Thomas Savage, Archbishop of York (see page 18) to purchase some of the Archbishop's lands so that income from rents etc. could provide a good salary for a Roman Catholic priest in Macclesfield, who would also be master of an intended grammar school.

This presumably gave the Archbishop the

Part of the school

The end looking toward the church

Adapted from a sketch in Birkenhead Library (said to be the only one in existence) of the Old Grammar School premises c.1553-1748, situated behind the parochial chapel (now St. Michael's Church) on Bunker's Hill.

At this time the building, to be known as the 'Free Grammar School of King Edward the Sixth in Macclesfield', must have been the one erected close to the northeastern corner of the chapel ground, at the top of Bunkers Hill. There it remained for almost 200 years.

Writing in 1747, an 18th century observer commented:

'I often wonder to fee a Man who can write his Name to a Note of Ten Thousand Pound, yet cannot dictate a common Letter of Bufinefs with any kind of Propriety of Language or write a Line free from falfe Grammer or bad Spelling'. He continued by attacking schools for spending too much time teaching Classics 'whatever Progrefs they made in Greek and Latin it is certain they often know no more of their Mother Tongue... than if they had been born in Japan or at the Cape of Good Hope'.

He insisted that his son should learn English Grammar thoroughly first and then 'a Trading Tongue' such as French or Dutch.

These were the sentiments close to the hearts of one or two Governors of the Macclesfield Grammar School which, by the 1740s, was totally inadequate for what they envisaged; in addition the building was old.

By that period the school, sited at the top of Bunker's Hill, was also being used for the production of plays and meetings which were attended by important and wealthy patrons and governors. The visitors passed to and fro in their carriages, suggesting that the northern part of Church Side was considerably wider than today.

The building appears to have been extended during its 200 years of existence. An old drawing shows a three storey construction at 'the end looking toward the church', with an additional two-storey extension added onto the northern end (or perhaps it was the other way round and the two-storey building was there first).

A Deed of 1544 refers to 'a tenement with a garden to the same, adjacent le Walgate (Church Street) between the chapell of All Saints in the town of Macclesfield on the West part and the water of Macclesfield (River Bollin) on the East . . .' This suggests that the tenement was either held in trust, or taken over and enlarged after the re-founding of 1552.

During 1748, a suitable property became available on Back Street (King Edward Street) and so it was possible to sell the old premises, on November 30th 1750, to a button merchant called Nathaniel Bradock, who is said to have converted them into a button manufactory.

* * *

Mr. Bradock borrowed money from one of the Hulley family – Jasper, whose wife, Mary, was sister to Thomas Hooley deceased (by whose will the Parish Church received a superb brass candelabrum and Derbyshire marble font). The premises 'known as the schoolhouse . . . and used as a workhouse for the manufacture of silk and mohair' also included a 'Dungpit' at the rear of the building, an 'asset' from the schooldays.

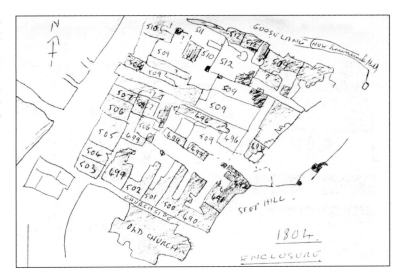

A rough sketch taken from the 1804 enclosure award showing a structure in the Market Place. Building No. 503 was the Old Guildhall, building no.505 occupied the site of The King's Oven where, for centuries, the residents of Macclesfield paid to have their bread and pies etc. baked.

Mr. Bradock, heavily in debt, died in 1762 leaving a widow and five children, one of whom was probably in partnership with David Hall as silk throwsters. The latter firm appeared on a Petition to Parliament in 1765 stating that they employed 360 persons in 1762, 260 in 1763 but only 20 in 1764, due to the depressed state of the silk trade.

The family interest was retained for several years until they were sued for debt in 1782. The situation was temporarily relieved by a large loan from John Hall (who could have been the son baptised by David Hall on July 26th. 1748 – St. Michael's Register) and circumstantial evidence suggests that between 1782 to 1785 the premises were converted into the Gutters Mill. (An early 19th century historian refers to Bradock and Hall of Churchside).

More and more loans were taken on until finally, in the Macclesfield Courier and Herald newspaper of July 4th 1812, an advert appeared: GUTTERS MILL 'To be let and entered upon immediately a silk factory situate on Bunker's Hill, in the centre of the town of Macclesfield, four storeys high, eighteen yards by seven yards wide, with a good horse-wheel attached.' This was one of the few mills in Macclesfield to be powered by a horse-gin.

* * *

For virtually the whole of the 18th century, the area of land between the old school premises and the top of the 108 steps (i.e. the greater part of Sparrow Park today) remained a piece of land in private ownership. The earliest deed for this area, dated April 3rd 1784, shows

the involvement of Thomas Holland, a bricklayer, and William Pierpoint of Rainow, yeoman, when the land was 'bought to be built upon'. It is possible, of course, that at some time it belonged to the school plot. By August 26th 1793, dwelling houses (or cottages) had been built and appear on an old postcard of Macclesfield, sometimes referred to in error as the old school premises. The land area, however, suggests an enclosure for cattle or animals in general, brought to the market either for sale, or slaughter by the butchers.

The Enclosure Award Plan, begun 1796, but published 1804, shows a structure in the Market Place divided into four parts. Could this signify enclosures for animals to replace the area at the top of the 108 Steps?

A Corporation meeting of October 2nd 1778 ordered 'that the Shops on the West Side of the Church Yard in the said Borough belonging to this Corporation and now in the occupation of Henry Hervey and Matthew Bayley be taken down'.

This infers that the shops originally built by Philomen Mainwaring (see page 11) had been acquired by the Mayor, Aldermen and Burgesses operating the next best thing to a Compulsory Purchase scheme. Instructions were given for the lowering of a wall 'to make it uniform with the Walls of the said Church Yard', thus opening up the view of St. Michael's from the Market Place.

The steps at the southern end of the shops had to be 'intirely taken away' and 'the Materials of the said shops sold to defray the Expence of the said Alteration'.

From Eleanor of Castile to the Black Prince

Duke William of Normandy and his host of 1066 were actually of Viking stock. Their French adoption had barely been completed before their arrival in England. Claiming the throne as William I, after Harold's defeat at Hastings, he then hoped for a peaceful take-over, but was forced to demonstrate his power against an uprising in Yorkshire, where large areas of the shire were laid waste. William immediately crossed the Pennines into Cheshire to build castles in Chester and Shrewsbury.

A scene from the Bayeux Tapestry depicting the Norman Conquest in 1066. The original was commissioned by William I's half brother Bishop Odo.

At this time, Macclesfield was one of the manors held by Earl Edwin of Mercia, but William granted the whole county to Gherbod, who shortly returned to Flanders, when it passed to William's nephew, Hugh. In 1071, Cheshire was made responsible for what was until recently most of modern Flintshire and Denbighshire, and Hugh, now Earl of Chester, was granted extensive power in return for military service against the Welsh.

Cheshire was in the unique position of having only two royal tenants, the Bishop and Earl Hugh. Although not above the law, it allowed the Earl some independence to give away land or retain it on his own terms, with very little contrivance. He also chose to preside in the County Court, as sheriffs of other counties did, thus giving the sheriffs of Cheshire a somewhat demoted position.

In 1086, William I commissioned the Domesday Survey, in which Cheshire appeared divided into seven areas called 'hundreds', the poorest of which was Macclesfield. At this time, the county was barren and sparsely populated. Records reveal poor climatic conditions, with many wet spells in the late 11th and early 12th centuries. The result was ruined harvests, plague and famine, with cattle disease and many animals drowned. The rivers Dee and Weaver were liable to flooding in their lower reaches, so the county was not the same lush green territory we see today.

(This is possibly why Macclesfield, at a later date, with its elevated position at the eastern side of the county, acquired a cattle farm supporting 'four vaccaries' by 1240 which, at its peak, grew to more than 700 head between 1354 and 1363.)

The 1086 survey records one mill only in the whole of the hundred viz: the one for Macclesfield manor 'to supply the Hall'. The manor, held by Robert Fitzhugh, had only 12 acres of sown land. Another tenant had 7 acres, indicating that the remainder of the area was either forest or waste, apart from a little sown land in Butley manor.

The incentive was, therefore, with the Earl to build up the county's resources. On his death, in 1101, the earldom passed to his son, then nephew, Ranulph (I) and continued within the family.

During 1230, an interesting episode took place when the then Earl, Ranulph (III), and the King, Henry III, visited Brittany, where Simon de Montfort, Ranulph's cousin, rightly claimed the earldom of Chester on behalf of his elder brother, in lieu of their father killed in battle. Ranulph agreed the claim and Henry supported, so Simon became an Englishman by adoption.

Meanwhile, Cheshire was developing, and many troops left the port of Chester for Ireland, or on occasion, for Carlisle, when there was trouble with the Scots.

Ranulph died in 1232, and the king settled the Earl's estates outside Cheshire amongst the co-heirs; however, he could not reinstate de Montfort to the earldom without too much upset, so he continued to pay Simon a pension of 400 marks p.a.

Ranulph's nephew, John the Scot, 8th Earl of Huntingdon, assumed the earldom.

Early in 1237, John fell ill and on May 13th, King Henry sent the Bishop of Coventry and Lichfield, together with Henry de Audley, to keep peace in the county. It seemed to be no secret that John was dying of poisoning (the culprit was alleged to be his wife). He died on June 6th without heirs, and Henry seized the county revenues, Chester Castle and the new castle at Beeston, but was legally unable to complete the land acquisitions.

It is no surprise that Simon de Montfort secretly married the king's widowed sister on January 7th 1238; the king gave away the bride. De Montfort also became godfather to Prince Edward.

In 1253, Henry had problems negotiating the marriage of Prince Edward to Eleanor, only daughter of Ferdinand III of Castile. However, on February 14th 1254 Edward, created Earl of Chester, was given a present of the whole county and the king's lands in North Wales.

Henry's problems had obviously been solved, for on November 1st 1254, Edward married Eleanor (by tradition, at the Cistercian convent of las Huegas near Burgos in Castile), and she, as part of the settlement, held the manor and forest of Macclesfield.

After her marriage, the princess – almost 16 years old (although recent research has suggested she was probably at least a year younger) – spent the next year in Gascony with

The stained glass window of Queen Eleanor in the Savage Chapel of St Michael's Church.

Edward, then travelled to Dover in October 1255.

Henry lll had decorated his daughter-in-law's apartments in the Spanish style. There were so many tapestries, even on the floors, that the citizens of London amusingly compared them with the inside of a church.

Eleanor's accounts reveal that on September 27th 1290, shortly before her death, she sent seven presents of cloth from London to 'Makelesfeud' with her trusted servant, Amisius, by means of two horses. The expenses were noted as two days before the arrival of the king in Macclesfield.

At her death six children were living, though she is said to have borne 15 or 16. She was a cultured woman of great intelligence who loved writing and discussing books, hunting and music, and gave generously to religious orders. Women were able to petition her personally, and from April 1289 until her death on November 28th 1290, she provided 9,306

The south door of St. Michael's, which is in the approximate position of the entrance to the original chapel founded by Queen Eleanor in 1278. The consecration cross is preserved on the stone to the right hand side of the door handle.

meals for paupers in the kingdom, much less than the king, but still very significant.

Eleanor took part in the Crusade of 1270-72 – in fact her daughter, Joanna, was born in Acre. She is said to have saved Edward's life by sucking poison from his wound after an assassination attempt. This account came via an Italian chronicler, from a country through which they passed on their return to England; other accounts ignore Eleanor and credit male companions. From the subsequent devotion of Edward to Eleanor the former version has more of a ring of truth to it.

Whilst in Acre (1272), Henry died and Edward I succeeded. In subsequent years, although the court continually moved around the English countryside, Queen Eleanor kept in constant touch with the family. She also corresponded with her bailiff, Thomas of Macclesfield.

The controller of her household, Richard de Bures, had at one time been bailiff of the manor and forest, but then Thomas must have proved himself trustworthy of such an important position.

Thomas of Macclesfield

The earliest known details relating to a Macclesfield will are those of Thomas de Macclesfield, dated 1301, and written in medieaval Latin. Together with various snippets, they reveal much information about the area and Thomas, two centuries after the Norman Conquest, but his early life still remains a mystery.

The position of Earl of Chester often entailed long absences due to periods of military service of the king, so initially, law and order were entrusted to eight 'lay' barons throughout Cheshire, all Norman.

It would seem, however, that previous Saxon overlords were still allowed a share of former holdings by convenient and peaceful integration: their offspring on occasion married Normans.

Gilbert de Venables of Kinderton (Middlewich) was the grandson of an original baron and had married Margaret, daughter of a Saxon who previously held Goostrey and Cranage. Their daughter, Amabilia, married Richard de Davenport who, by a grant from the Earl of Chester (c.1166) held the important position of Chief Forester of Macclesfield.

Amabilia received a gift of property from her brother, to use as her share of the marriage settlement, which was witnessed by several influential men with Norman names and one, Gilbert, son of Nigell. The latter suggests a Saxon origin, an important man who was more than likely Thomas of Macclesfield's ancestor.

Millicent, his wife's name, was of French origin but became popular in England in the late 1100s. At present, nothing is known of her family. (Subsequent information has disclosed some interesting details, which will be revealed below).

In 1274, during a legal wrangle, Thomas was described as 'clerk'. The matter concerned land enclosures in the forest at Hurdsfield, and Thomas was taken to court in Northampton where Macclesfield Burgesses claimed that 6 acres belonged to them. They won. This indicates that Thomas was not a burgess but Clerk of the Manor and Forest Court (Halmote), otherwise a court in Cheshire would have been used for the hearing.

The fact that Thomas held a legal position meant that he had been well educated by monks or Templars. He later sent his son, Jordan, to Oxford where he obtained his M.A., having studied both Canon and Civil law. Thomas obviously intended his son to follow in his footsteps.

Macclesfield was becoming an important religious centre after the foundation of the chapel by Queen Eleanor on the anniversary of her wedding, i.e. 1st November 1278, which must have made the chapel very special and close to the Queen's heart. It was, of course, the day of All Hallows or All Saints, to which the chapel was dedicated.

At his death, Thomas willed money to the Carmelite friars of Chester, one of whom was his son, Robert, and also to the singing and minor monks of Chester and Shrewsbury (i.e. Dominicans and Fransicans respectively). The latter donation is interesting because the Venables family had given land to the Shrewsbury monks.

Thomas also left three 'good' hangings or curtains, one to Macclesfield Chapel and two to the church of Lichfield. It is tempting to think that these were part of the seven pieces of cloth which Queen Eleanor had sent to Macclesfield shortly before her death in 1290, particularly as Thomas had progressed from clerk to the prestigious position of Eleanor's personal bailiff, not only of Macclesfield Manor and Forest, but also of the Manor of Overton, Flintshire.

At Overton, he kept three horses for riding,

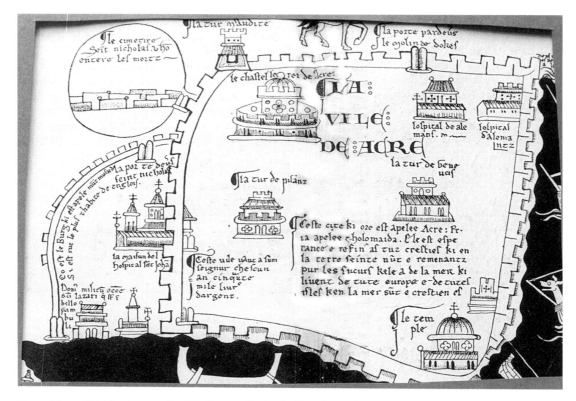

Map of Acre. This city, just north of Haifa, was the foothold in the Holy Land for the Crusaders.

but in Macclesfield he had two for riding, together with a packhorse which went with him through the forest, and one which he had permission to use across the parkland. The park officially still belonged to the king, because here the animals were kept to sustain any armies necessary for campaigns in Scotland, Ireland and Wales, and were under the watchful eye of the park keeper, known as a 'parker'.

At the far end of the park, Thomas had acres of sown land near Gawsworth, which were sufficient to engage two ploughs. His Hurdsfield enclosures held 120 sheep, 36 cows, 12 young bullocks, 30 oxen and 10 pigs.

The extent of his jurisdiction can be judged by the fact that he was Lord of Stayley (Stavelegh) manor near Mottram-in-Longdendale, where he would need to stay occasionally after his long trek from Macclesfield. There, he kept a considerable number of sheep and ten oxen.

Thomas must have been a strong, powerful man, both in mind and body who, at Eleanor's death, was allowed to retain his bailiwick for the considerable sum of £220. He loved hawking and left several pairs of young birds to friends and relatives and an aviary to one of his

daughter's sons. Amongst other gifts was his green tunic and red robe.

Thomas was a very religious man. Eleanor would not have had it otherwise. He left orders for his wife to provide vestments of gold cloth for the Macclesfield priest – an expensive gift. He was also obliged to leave the priest his best beast (usually a horse) in payment for his funeral, but in addition, he left a cow to the Dean as chief coffin bearer, and six pence to the other bearers, who would also sing and chant.

On 1st October 1290, Eleanor had sent 13 shillings and 4 pence for clothes for the 'Anchorite de makelesfeld', Thomas also left 40 pence for the 'recluse de Macclisfeud': this was presumably the same person.

Recluse or Anchorite

The previous century had seen a religious revival, with many copying the lives of saints. Recluses lived in woods and forests, either in huts or caves, but some preferred places known as cells, or a hermitage attached to a religious building. Some cultivated waste lands, kept roads and bridges in repair, and acted as guides in difficult and dangerous areas.

The Macclesfield recluse more than likely lived in a cell on the more austere north side of the chapel, although a few lived under the eaves of churches. A Bavarian rule stipulated a room of 12ft square, with a window towards the choir through which Holy Communion was received, another through which food was handed in and one with glass through which a lantern shone.

An anchorite chose this more austere life for penitence or dedication and, if a woman, could open the door connecting with the church, but was concealed by a black curtain bearing a white cross.

The fact that St. Michael's Church has been enlarged on the northern side at different periods, could account for the lack of evidence of such a cell. At this early date, neither the Legh nor the Savage chapels had been built.

Deaths and burials

Deaths and burials hold a fascination for many people. From the historical view point, paradoxically they reveal much about the living, often with surprising results.

One historian wrote of Eleanor of Castile, 'hers is not a personality that stands out from the pages of the records or the chronicles'. With regard to Macclesfield this is certainly not true. I suspect that her influence on, and her devotion to her husband, Edward I, are far greater than first appears.

Edward's grief at her death inspired the construction of three tombs; one at Lincoln for her entrails, one, by her own wish, for her heart in the Lady Chapel of the Dominican priory at Blackfriars, London, and the main one, bearing her effigy, in Westminster Abbey. In addition there was the erection of the Eleanor Crosses – an elaborate series of monuments – twelve in all, marking each resting place of her corpse from Nottinghamshire (she is now known to have died at Harby in Leicestershire) to her final entombment. No other king or queen of England has received such commemoration.

Although division of the corpse was usual at this time, Pope Bonaface VIII legislated against it in 1299, apparently creating a new custom. When Thomas of Macclesfield died in 1303 his

A Victorian print depicting a forest hermit, and also a knight in 15th century armour.

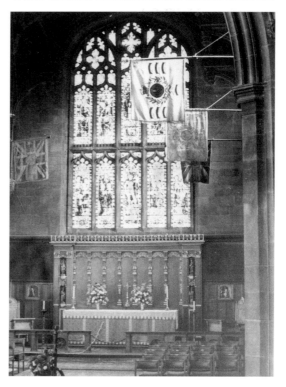

The main altar of St. Michael's parish church today. A second smaller altar now occupies a site in the Savage Chapel, which was originally intended for the Earl Rivers monument (photograph on page 18).

will stipulated that his body had to be entombed before the Altar of the Blessed Virgin in Macclesfield chapel and mentioned his heart mortuary. A Mortuary badge was generally heart shaped. A 15th century will mentions a 'broche herte of gold to be hange, naylyd and festnyd upon the shryne'. So although tradition says that in the early 16th century the heart of Thomas Savage, Archbishop of York, was brought to Macclesfield and placed in the wall of the Savage Chapel, perhaps nothing barbaric occurred, and only a representation of the real thing arrived!

According to Thomas of Macclesfield's will only two altars were built, i.e. the High Altar and the Altar of the Blessed Virgin. This seems to apply to other churches at that period e.g. Prestbury, Astbury etc. where other wealthy benefactors requested burial before 'oure Lady's aulter'.

About 1361 Randle Whylof died. Amongst other things he held a third share interest in the manorial mill of Macclesfield. He was buried in Prestbury and, apart from his gifts to the church there, he made several donations to the Macclesfield chapel. In addition to the two original altars there was a new one and another dedicated to the Holy Trinity; the latter strongly suggesting the influence of the Black Prince.

The celebration of Holy Trinity was known as early as the 10th century, but it took some time to spread throughout the churches of Northern Europe, until finally Pope John XXII (1316-34) approved it for the entire Catholic Church. It is still celebrated on the Sunday following Pentecost (the great Jewish Feast) also known as Whitsunday in the Christian Church.

The Black Prince, one of the original Knights of the Garter, held this relatively new festival in special honour, and a lead 'badge' with a border representing the garter, portrays him worshipping the Trinity; it was, in fact his birthday. By strange coincidence he also died (naturally) on Trinity Sunday (1376). His visits to Macclesfield during the 1350s must have influenced the dedication of this altar.

Female Saints

Randle Whytlof also left money for the support of three shrines in addition to the altars. Each would have a wax image of its saint. One for Mary Magdalene, the first witness of Christ's resurrection; the other two, far less known today, for Katherine and Margaret.

St. Katherine of Alexandria was tortured on a wheel in 307 A.D. and, although her Feast Day is 25th November, sadly she should be remembered on the 5th of the month, as the famous Catherine wheel firework is named after her.

St. Margaret guarded mothers in childbirth and was still revered by mass in the 18th century. She was Queen of Scotland and had been brought up at the court of Edward the Confessor. Described as 'a woman of beautiful character and great piety' she did much to 'civilize the country by her devotion and example'. She was canonised by Pope Innocent IV in 1250; so again it would have been a relatively new Feast

The Parish Church of St. Michael and All Angels: its history is inextricably linked with the town of Macclesfield.

Day (10th June or 16th November).

This devotion to female saints certainly implies inspiration from Queen Eleanor, as does Edward's crusade to Acre 1270-72 and his foundation of Vale Royal Abbey, which was planned to be the largest Cistercian house in England. The ceremony took place in August 1277, shortly before that of the Macclesfield chapel, but suddenly in 1290 the king announced he was no longer concerned with the abbey and would have nothing further to do with the building. Was it just coincidence that this was the year of Eleanor's death?

By the time the Macclesfield schoolmaster, William Bridges, prepared his will in March 1536 the female influence had well and truly gone. During almost two centuries the 'Age of Chivalry' had left its mark. The 'hie aultaer' and 'oure Ladyes aulter' remained, but a further altar had been added, dedicated to 'the Holis Rhodes', and the other two rededicated to St. James. The Holy Rhodes altar, (perhaps a rood-altar behind the rood screen, but the spelling is an unusual alternative), may refer to the incredible seige of the Island of Rhodes by Suleiman's Turkish army.

Seige of Rhodes

The Knights Hospitallers, original carers of sick pilgrims to the Holy Land and members of the Order of St. John of Jerusalem, had been forced to flee Acre for Cyprus when Jerusalem fell. This was not a good move, but in 1307, having rid Rhodes of its pirates, they settled on the island.

The 15th century saw incredible efforts on the part of the Moslems to remove them. but to no avail. After a final bitter struggle of many months, Suleiman allowed the Grand Master and survivors to leave in peace, under the terms of a truce dated 26th December 1522, as a mark of his respect and admiration for them.

Pilgrimage

The two altars to St. James (the Great) must surely indicate that pilgrims from the Macclesfield area had made the compelling pilgrimage to his shrine in Northern Spain at Santiago de Compostela.

The 'mystery' maintains that James, unable to convert Spain to Christianity returned to the Holy Land but was beheaded and his body thrown to the dogs. His remains were gathered by two disciples and returned to Spain for burial. In 814 relics were found by Bishop Theodomir and the cult began. After the Moors' defeat of 1492 in Granada, pilgrims surged across Europe to Santiago.

The Spanish connection was further encouraged by Queen Mary's marriage to Philip of Spain in 1554, but in spite of Elizabeth I's enmity with the country 'Spanish sylke buttons' began to appear on early 17th century inventories in Macclesfield.

Effigy of Edward of Woodstock, Prince of Wales, also Earl of Chester and Duke of Cornwall, apparently referred to as 'The Black Prince' in the first instance by the Victorians.

Macclesfield forest

The importance of Macclesfield forest to the development of Macclesfield Town, in fact, to the very existence of the township, cannot be over-emphasised.

Although Queen Eleanor left her own special mark here with the foundation of a chapel and small religious community, yet this complemented the already well-established vigorous administration of the forest by the Normans. Unfortunately, with the death of the bailiff, Thomas of Macclesfield in 1303, his son Jordan, who appears to have been a much weaker character, faced many problems.

Another death, that of Edward I in 1307, saw Macclesfield forest pass into the hands of Queen Isabel from 1309, until it was exchanged for two of her grandson's manors. Meanwhile many encroachments and damage had taken place and those with privileges to hunt game had taken advantage.

Grandson Edward, born at his mother, Philippa's favourite palace of Woodstock in Oxfordshire on Trinity Sunday, 15th June 1330 was only 17 years old when he acquired Macclesfield manor and forest. The previous year the young Prince of Wales had led the vanguard of 4,000 men at Crécy where the English army was outnumbered 3 to 1. Under his command were experienced warriors, including Sir John Chandos, and 2,000 archers. Sir John, described as 'courteous, skilled and true' was to become a loyal and devoted friend to the prince.

In 1353 concern over disturbances saw Edward pay his first visit to Cheshire, and Sir John was created 'master forester and surveyor of the Cheshire forests' and given a grant for 'putting them in better condition'.

There could have been two other reasons; a strong character was needed to solve the problems of the forests of Wirhale (Wirral) and Macclesfield, the latter experiencing many skirmishes thanks to Adam de Mottram, bailiff and

A falconer. Macclesfield foresters were entitled to hawks and eagles (falcons) in the forest. They hunted quail and partridge with the help of their birds of prey and spaniels.

keeper of the gaol, and Robert de Foxwist one of the foresters, who were not very popular men. Secondly a genuine desire to assess and keep in mind the value of the Cheshire archers, having proved their worth at Crécy.

Sir Perkin Legh had been given Lyme as an estate for serving well Edward III and his son, the Black Prince, in that campaign. The Black Prince certainly intended further campaigns and 'the best and most skilful archers of Cheshire' were to be tested and arrayed. Apparently there were few in Wirral forest, but a large contingent from Macclesfield Hundred was chosen amongst others, and dispatched to Plymouth with Sir John Hide, from where they eventually gained honours at Poitiers. It was during this battle that Chandos saved the Black Prince's life.

Prince Edward's concern for his Cheshire forests during his absence was very genuine. He had previously issued rules for the forests, to all concerned, in March 1351. On 2nd July 1355 instructions were sent to Robert de Legh, steward and forester of Macclesfield 'the prince would hate his game to be destroyed or ruined in any way during his absence beyond (the) seas'.

Macclesfield Forest was overseen by eight foresters responsible to Sir John and his deputy, Legh. Each held office 'by service of carrying a horn' which at this time was a curved hunting horn made from a horn of an animal. Some were decorated with gold and silver rings and mouthpieces, occasionally one had a stopper for conversion into a drinking horn. They varied in length from 18 inches to 2ft (approx. $\frac{1}{2}$ to $\frac{2}{3}$ metre).

Forest management was based on French hunting laws which gave priority to preservation and conservation of the environment. These had been adopted by the Normans and were disciplines which they had brought with them at the time of the Conquest in 1066.

A French hunting book, later translated by Edward, nephew of the Black Prince, clearly indicates which animals remained in the English forests more than 300 years after the advent of the Normans. Edward omits only four: reindeer, chamois (including the ibex), bear and, surprisingly, rabbits. Favourite for the chase was the hare, which together with foxes and others was considered vermin and hunted all year round. Next came the hart, buck and roe-deer but only in the appropriate season, with breeding carefully respected and selected mature animals killed.

During the prince's visit to Chester Sir John Chandos was sent an order on 10th August 1353 'to cause six roes to be taken quickly in the said forest (Mackelesfeld) without frightening the other beasts of the forest there and to send them to Cestre by Wednesday next'.

Wild boar, like deer, were also hunted for food and sport made out of it. Wolves were hunted, not only for the danger to livestock but also to human beings; one is reminded of the man-eating tigers of India. The mediaeval wolf was an extremely large strong animal that could easily kill a cow or mare, and its jaws had such power that it was known to have carried off a goat, sheep or even young hogs. Young wolves reared near battlefields or gallows, the latter having corpses hanging too near the ground, unfortunately acquired a taste for tender human flesh. Occasionally it happened that a shepherd would be dragged away and killed, leaving his flock untouched!

It is easy, therefore, to understand Prince Edward's concern when issuing orders for the trapping of wolves in the forest and offering a reward when the ears were produced as evidence of a kill.

Normally in England hunting was done with 'running hounds' (the best kind considered as 'of a hue brown tan') and greyhounds; trapping was used more on the Continent. Hounds were highly revered and had to be kept in good condition by hunting two or three times each week.

On 13th September 1358 Sir John Chandos was made steward of Longdendale, responsible for keeping and supervising the prince's chase. A pack of hounds would have been kept there and trained, as were the four pair in the 'coombes' near Shutlingslow, for which John de Donvill was given two plots of land for 'providing a huntsman to follow the prince's hounds when he hunts the coombes'.

In 1360 Sir John was in France having been appointed the King of England's regent and lieutenant there. By 4th December 1361 the prince threatened to remove the Macclesfield foresters from office and seize their lands unless they were 'diligent and persistent', as he had learnt of the 'great loss and damage to vert and venison' in the forest of Macclesfield.

Goose Lane – The Flying Childers

The name Goose Lane conjures up idyllic scenes of English rural life. Renamed Brunswick Street at the time of the Napoleonic Wars, today the land on its northern side is owned by the Cheshire County Council.

As its name implies, the lane in the 18th century contained dwelling houses, cottages with outbuildings, gardens and land, and two of these properties, eventually numbered 18 and 20 Brunswick Street, occupied the site of the new police station.

A Victorian O.S. map circa 1870 shows a public house called the Childers at No.12, later renamed the Feathers. Today its site neatly fits between the end of the new extension, built to enlarge the Old District Bank building for use as a new Public Library, and the main building of the Cheshire Constabulary. In fact it must have occupied the area now covered by the police kennels in which stray dogs are kept.

Part of Brunswick Street, originally named Goose Lane. On the right the Cheshire Constabulary, site of two former cottages with gardens etc. In the middle was the approximate site of the Flying Childers Inn adjacent to the extension of the new library.

The unusual name of Childers has an interesting explanation. At Carr Hall near Doncaster in 1715 Leonard Childers bred what was to become, 'The first truly great racehorse' – the *Flying Childers*.

At an early age the horse was sold to the Duke of Devonshire and, together with the painting, the original certificate still exists at Chatsworth House, which reads 'Sept. ye 28 1719. This is to certify that the bay stoned Horse his Grace the Duke of Devonshire bought of me, was bred by me, and was five years old last grass, and no more. Witness my hand, Leo Childers.'

The horse must have been purchased by the 2nd Duke who died in 1729, and then inherited by his son, the 3rd Duke. He was an M.P. from 1721 (during his father's lifetime), a great friend of the Prime Minister, Sir Robert Walpole, and later served as Lord Lieutenant of Ireland for seven years. Incidentally it was thanks to the intervention of this Duke that the famous composer, Handel, after having been accused of pirating other composers' works, was offered a series of concerts in Ireland.

Tradition maintains that Handel finished his 'Messiah' at Adlington Hall near Macclesfield whilst staying with the Legh family in the spring of 1742, from where he performed a brief but unsuccessful rehearsal of it in Chester. However, its first public performance in Dublin on 13th April produced such a profound impression that its success was assured.

The success of the *Flying Childers*, known also as the *Devonshire Childers*, and even Childers for a short period, was also assured. He first ran in April 1721 and beat the Duke of Bolton's horse, *Speedwell* over 4 miles, winning 500 guineas (at least £55,000 today) and then beat the Earl of Drogheda's *Chanter* in October of that year over 6 miles for 1,000 guineas. Both races took place at Newmarket where observers considered him to be the fastest horse they had ever seen.

Flying Childer's invincible reputation was established. Incredibly, although two further races were arranged 'his intended adversaries declared forfeit on each occasion' so he remained unbeaten and stood as a stallion at the Duke's stables, Chatsworth until his death in 1741.

He covered very few mares except those of the Duke, and although he did not found an enduring male line, opinions agree that his influence on the breed was profound. One of his sons *Snip*, only a moderate race horse, did sire a very successful stallion, appropriately called *Snap*, which ran unbeaten in the 1750s.

Flying Childers resembled his sire, the *Darley Arabian*, being bay with much white on his legs

Painting of *Flying Childers* attributed to James Seymour. The photograph provided by the Courtauld Institute of Art and permission for reproduction, together with details of the horse's original certificate, have kindly been given by the Trustees of the Devonshire Collection, Chatsworth and Mr. P Day, the former Keeper of Collections there.

and face. The question of his dam, however, arouses great disputes amongst Turf historians. If the official General Stud Book is taken as correct then *Flying Childers* came from imported Eastern horses with no indigenous English strains, but a prominent early 18th century breeder disputed this, and the question now seems beyond a solution.

Such was the enthusiasm for breeding racehorses that anyone would be forgiven for thinking it was encouraged – but far from it. In 1740 an Act of Parliament was passed to prevent the 'excessive Increase of Horse Races' and considered that 'the Breed of strong and useful Horses hath been much prejudiced'. Horses were judged to be useful working animals and not for frivolous pursuits.

A further Act of 1745 to contain games of cards, dice and Roulet, was appended 'and to restrain and prevent the excessive Increase of Horse Races'. Too late came the cry, although officially there was, for some considerable time, a restriction for allowing a person one racehorse only. In the early days of racing big weights were carried long distances, so a racehorse developed slowly and did not run until mature.

It is difficult to judge the speed of *Flying Childers*, whose stride is claimed as 25ft.

His calculated speed for both Newmarket races is 33/34 miles per hour respectively, although modern experts express doubts. Today the 2¾ miles distance at Ascot is the longest flat race in England, producing average speeds of 33 miles per hour by modern racehorses.

Whatever his capabilities Flying Childers must have been exceptional, and the house and brewhouse named after him on Goose Lane must have been in existence for some considerable time, possibly from the early 18th century.

These premises became the meeting place for the Freemasons' Lodge No. 189 of the Ancients from 1774 to 1794. About this time there were three Masonic Lodges in town, all evidently with early military connections, and it seems strange that the Duke of Devonshire Lodge had not appropriated the *Flying Childers* for its own meetings.

Sometimes referred to in the deeds as the *Childers*, the premises passed into the possession of Saville Smith on 15th June 1824, He is listed in the 1825 Macclesfield Directory as landlord of 'The Flying Childers Brunswick Street'.

Today there is still a pub at Stanton-in-the-Peak, Derbyshire named *Flying Childers*, and an annual race at Doncaster, not Newmarket, dedicated to his memory.

Bonnie Prince Charlie

A quarter of a millennium ago Macclesfield was about to be invaded for the last time. The culprit, of course, was to be Bonnie Prince Charlie, and much has been written, both truth and legend, about this extraordinary chapter of English history.

Fortunately a recent biography helps set the record straight. Susan Maclean Kybett, herself Scottish and brought up on the Isle of Lewis, where the Prince had sought help all those years ago, is to be admired for her determination in researching almost 17,000 letters and documents in English, French, Italian, Latin and Spanish held in Windsor Castle. At last much is revealed about a hitherto elusive character.

Although the book is excellent in content only a brief mention of the incursion into England is made, so Local History can prevail. Nevertheless a brief background description is essential to put the episode into perspective.

Henry VIII in his efforts to divorce his first

The Prince in his early thirties by Jean-Louis Tocqué from the collection of the Duke of Atholl, Blair Castle, Blair Atholl, Perthshire. At the time of his arrival in Macclesfield Prince Charles was almost 25 years old.

wife, Catherine of Aragon, is said to have rid England of Roman Catholicism, but Henry was playing a much more complicated game. The Roman Catholic Church of Tudor times was very different from today and highly political. Politicians need money and the Pope was no exception, extracting tithes from monasteries and other religious establishments far beyond the boundaries of Rome.

Every year a great deal of English wealth was carried to Rome as tithe payments, so Henry decided enough was enough and established a Church of England.

Henry used his new source of income to build ships which competed for trade with the Roman Catholic powers of Europe. When James II came to the throne in 1685 he failed to understand the situation and taking advice from Jesuit priests, caused much upset.

James had two Protestant daughters by his first marriage, Mary and Anne, who in turn succeeded him, but neither left heirs. Meanwhile, after the death of his first wife, James had married Mary of Modena, a fervent Roman Catholic who, to everyone's surprise, in December 1687 announced she was pregnant. Princess Anne, highly suspicious, endeavoured to be with the Queen whenever she was disrobing.

On 10th June 1688 twenty nine Protestant and Catholic men and women witnessed the birth of James Francis Edward Stuart. Yet, in spite of this, a rumour circulated that he was really the child of a chambermaid smuggled into the Queen's bed in a warming pan, which took several months to contradict.

By this birth the politics of Europe were thrown into turmoil; James did not help by blatantly celebrating Mass and, amongst other things, placing Roman Catholics in positions of power in Ireland and Scotland. Our history books complete the story – the arrival of Mary's husband, William of Orange in Torbay, Devon 1688 and the rapid exodus of James II, Mary and young James to France.

Eighteen months later Louis XIV financed

the first failed restoration attempt and, still in exile, James died in 1701. He had written much for the benefit of young James regarding kingly power and the Church of Rome etc. and thus encouraged, his son appealed to Queen Anne for his rightful place on the English throne; he did not realise that Parliament had control over the succession.

In 1707 the union between England and Scotland took place and whilst Lowland Scots had no objections, the Highlanders were furious. They had a patriarchal clan system with each clan led by a chieftain and made up of members with common ancestors; even the Scottish government in Edinburgh had problems – the Highlanders were a law unto themselves.

During 1708, misjudging the situation, Louis XIV sent James to Scotland with 5,000 soldiers and 28 ships, but the voyage was a fiasco and Queen Anne, in a rage, placed a price on the head of the 'Pretender'. The name stuck.

The year following Queen Anne's death saw intrigues once more and another attempt at

Cumberland House, Jordangate. This is the only part of the building which dates back to at least the mid-18th century. John Stafford saw Bonnie Prince Charlie 'just opposite to my door for a minute or two...'

restoration, but again the Jacobites failed. Sophia, cousin of James II and wife of the Elector of Hanover, had a son, Prince George who, after much argument, was offered the English throne, becoming George I.

In 1719, James the Pretender, married Clementina, granddaughter of John III a famous Polish king, and settled in Rome at the Palazzo Muti, courtesy of the Pope, who assured him that as James III of England he would be given full royal honours.

Clementina had a son on 31st December 1720, christened Charles Edward Louis John Sylvester Maria Casimir – alias Bonnie Prince Charlie! Incidentally, as the calendar in the British Isles was not adjusted until 1752, we were still 11 days ahead of Europe but the Scots celebrated the birth on the 20th.

Although his father engaged English tutors, some Protestant, and built up Charles' hopes of becoming King of England, yet Charles was lazy and awkward. He became renowned for his love of beautiful expensive clothes and so it was that John Stafford, Clerk of the Manor and Forest of Macclesfield, saw him standing on Jordangate 'just opposite to my door for a minute or two . . . in Highland dress with a blue waistcote trim'd with silver, and had a blue Highland cap on'. (He was later to enter Derby wearing a green bonnet laced with gold.)

John Stafford's comment 'and walks well . . . He walked on foot from Manchester as he had done 'tis said all the way from Carlisle' is worth noting. As part of Charles' upbringing in Rome he had an excellent tutor, a priest, who taught him the art of survival in the roughest terrain, an attribute which appealed greatly to his Highland followers.

Details of the Highlanders' stay in Macclesfield are mostly taken from a letter written by John Stafford, but to whom? The letter devised by an extremely clever lawyer, is meticulously detailed. Every significant action on both sides is recorded, together with careful calculations of enemy numbers, arms and equipment, and was in response to one he had received warning him of the approaching Jacobite army from Manchester. His concluding words 'your humble servant J.S.' leaves little doubt that he was reporting to his superior, the Earl of Derby, whose estate was near Preston.

The Earl, having jurisdiction of the Manor and Forest of Macclesfield on behalf of the Crown, was directly responsible to the King for its law and order. John Stafford therefore would be anxious to ensure that no accusations of treason would take place in the aftermath of the Jacobite retreat from the Macclesfield area.

* * *

Prince Charles Edward Stuart had actually been smuggled out of Rome by his father James, the Old Pretender, in January 1745, en route for Paris. James had no intention of effecting another restoration attempt and neither had Louis XV, having succeeded his grandfather to the throne of France. It was purely a political move involving legitimate claims which James felt he had in recognition of his title 'James VIII of Scotland, III of Ireland and England, AND King of France.' The Scottish Royal House of Stuart for centuries had intermarried with the French royal family.

Charles however seized his opportunity. Free from the restrictions in Rome, he foolishly and arrogantly decided to act on his own and make a daring attempt to claim the English throne for his father. He worked secretly and quietly, much to the astonishment of his father and the consternation of Louis XV when they learnt too late of his plans, by which time he had sailed out of Nantes in the *Doutelle (Du Teillay)* and on the 12th July was waiting to be joined by a well armed privateer, the *Elizabeth*.

Thanks to the intervention of a British warship, the *Elizabeth*, although managing to regain the French coast, was badly damaged, but the Prince and seven companions were able to continue to Scotland aboard the *Doutelle*.

Many of his father's old supporters rallied to his cause bringing family members with them. In just six months Edinburgh was captured, the English army defeated at Prestonpans and, by the 12th November, the Prince was at the gates of Carlisle leading a substantial army. He really had no chance of success, but his victory at Prestonpans gave him the idea that he was invincible. Events were moving rapidly, he had taken everyone by surprise.

Unfortunately the mayor of Carlisle didn't help. He was a member of the Backhouse family from the North East, which suggests he was a Quaker and pacifist so, having received an ultimatum and with a fast dwindling population, he persuaded the Corporation to capitulate.

The town clerk, whose stepfather was a captain in the English army, abstained from the vote which let in the rebels. When the Duke of Cumberland's army eventually arrived in Carlisle, following the retreating Jacobites, Corporation members were immediately arrested, sent to London and imprisoned. As soon as details were known, the town clerk was given his freedom, but the mayor and others paid the price of their votes by further imprisonment.

* * *

The greatest problem faced by Charles and his army was that of feeding themselves. His father, still in Rome, and King Louis of France had now decided to back the enterprise (each for very different reasons) by sending money and arms via Scotland.

Numbers were difficult to calculate, as John Stafford discovered on their arrival in Macclesfield. 'They bespoke billets for 10,000, and said 5,000 would come in the next day but for my own part I don't think they exceed 6,000 in the whole.

The Prince had formed a council which included the Duke of Perth, Lord Elcho and Lord George Murray, but the latter was not liked by the Prince. The Duke of Perth was Roman Catholic which upset the Highlanders so, as the march progressed more and more arguments occurred with each council of war, one of which was held in Macclesfield. Lord David Elcho, son of the 5th Earl of Wemyss, had first met the 'Young Pretender' when visiting Rome and later was to become extremely critical of the way in which the Prince treated the Scottish nobility. Elcho headed 'a handsome body of horse guards' in red and blue uniforms, which must have been particularly striking as they are mentioned in various accounts.

John Stafford initially missed this regiment because he hesitated to see the troops pass his door and later wrote 'seeing my wife and her two sisters below at the Gates shame roused my courage and I ventured to stand by 'em, and saw the whole army pass by my own door, except a regiment of Horse commanded by Lord Elcho, and some forces which came later'.

Lord Elcho must have arrived first to give a good impression to the townspeople. He always led the first division and the Prince, the second.

One young Lowlander, who took up quarters with John Stafford and his family, said 'Manchester was a glorious town'.

The Prince had lost many men by desertion on his march from Carlisle to Manchester, but he expected and received a warm welcome

Above left: To the left of this picture stood the Market Cross where James III was declared King of England. The area shown was still part of Jordangate Street in the 18th century. **Above right:** A Staffordshire figure known as Bonnie Prince Charlie c.1895. The Gondola obviously represents the Italian connection but the boatman is typically British. Flora Macdonald is easily recognised however, the only portrait of the Prince available to the potter must have been that painted by Louis Gabriel Blanchet, now in the National Gallery, London. The portrait is of a young boy, left hand on hip, with a long drape around his waist and right hand resting on a plumed helmet. The potter has conveniently adapted the details and invented the buffet.

there and an additional 200 to 300 volunteers. It was later discovered that many of these were unemployed and had decided to enlist for whichever army arrived first!

John Stafford was surprised to see several old men and young boys amongst the troops, some shabbily dressed without breeches, stockings or shoes. The boys were to be used against the King's Cavalry for 'going amongst the ranks and cutting the legs of the horses'.

En route they had taken black cattle and sheep, driving them along the old Roman road (A6) from Penrith to Kendal. By tradition, when news of the fall of Carlisle came, Lakeland families gathered as many sheep and cattle as possible into a remote valley, well hidden from Jacobite eyes.

The Jacobites stayed three nights in Manchester from where, on Saturday evening, an advance guard went to Stockport and distributed leaflets around the Market Cross, hoping to encourage further volunteers to join them.

Sampson Salt, a grocer of Mill St. Macclesfield was sent to Stockport as a spy but, as he did not return quickly, the Corporation wrongly assumed that the army intended staying in Manchester a day or so longer.

The Prince had learnt some vital information in Manchester and anxiously hurried to Macclesfield. On arrival 'the quarter masters with their guard enquired for Sir P. Davenport's house' on hearing he was not in town they cursed, rode to his house 'and viewing it inside and out, marked the door with the word "PRINCE".' Here Bonnie Prince Charlie stayed.

Recent historians have suggested that Davenport was a Jacobite, that he certainly was not. He was important to the Prince because he was a Commissary in H.M. Forces, experienced in providing food and equipment for large numbers of soldiers. Either from sheer good luck or, I suspect, deliberately, Sir Peter was absent at that time.

The Jacobite army stayed in Macclesfield from Sunday to Tuesday 1st to 3rd December 1745. For many people they were the longest three days they would ever remember.

The previous Saturday night (30th November) a small group of Dragoons had arrived to gather information about the rebel army and report to the Duke of Cumberland, who was hurriedly approaching from the south. Sunday morning saw the young Dragoon officer enjoying breakfast with the Mayoress. He was just saying: 'Never fear Ma'am we'll protect you', when word arrived that the Jacobites were only a quarter of a mile from town. 'Down went his dish and he and his party of Dragoons made full as much haste out of the town as Madame Frances did'!

Consternation knew no bounds. The congregation attending morning service at St.

Michael's rushed out half way through, as Jacobite Regiments of Foot in full Highland Dress, marched up Jordangate, bagpipes playing.

Just ahead of this was the advance Guard commanded by James Drummond, Duke of Perth (a Jacobite title not officially recognised): he would die the following year from a chest ailment whilst escaping to France. As he was a Roman Catholic, under him marched a contingent of Irishmen amongst whom appeared 'four terrible fellows with their drawn swords', guarding a prisoner – none other than Sampson Salt, the grocer of Mill St. Macclesfield who had been sent to Stockport as a spy to report on the progress of the rebels. Poor Sampson was so terrified that at first no-one recognised him; struck dump, he dare not look left or right, and was made a figure of ridicule by the soldiers, who soon learnt he was from Macclesfield.

Efforts were made to find the team of bell ringers, yet only four could be persuaded to ring a peal of bells 'for fear of insults', but through confusion 'they rung the Bells backwards, not with design'.

Jordangate House, formerly Pear Tree House. Presumably the one referred to by John Stafford when he stepped 'over the way to a poor neighbour's house who had above 50 common men quartered upon him . . .'

On arrival the Prince 'took up his quarters' in the empty Davenport House on Back Street (now King Edward Street); which occupied the site immediately in front of the roundabout at the top of Churchill Way. Word was then sent to the Mayor and Aldermen to proclaim the Old Pretender, King James III of England, in a ceremony at the Market Cross, which the Town Clerk was forced to repeat. The artillery arrived after dark, when orders were given to all Macclesfield inhabitants to 'illuminate their houses upon pain of military execution'.

John Stafford, having spent an uncomfortable night, not with the young Lowlander billeted there, who turned out to be quite a gentleman, but with an unsavoury character who arrived later, walked out early feeling concern for his neighbours. He stepped 'over the way (? Jordangate House) to a poor neighbour's house who had above 50 common men quartered on him, to see how they lay. The house floor was covered in straw, and men, women, and children lay promiscuously together like a kennel of hounds, and some of 'em stark naked. As soon as it was daylight the streets appeared in Edinburgh fashion'. A great many common soldiers relieved themselves on the pavements, much to the disgust of the poor Maxonians!

John Stafford, having obtained permission to take his family and others to Shrigley, left his clerks and servants guarding the house. Come the next day, Tuesday, he hurried home 'with great joy' having learnt that the Jacobites were leaving. However, nearing Macclesfield he was told that some troops had returned to burn down the town as one of their number had been wounded. The incident had taken place in premises occupying the corner site of Chestergate and the Market Place, adjacent the Angel Inn (today part of the NatWest bank site).

The property was a house and shop occupied by Samuel Burgess in 1742. Described as being erected on the site of 'an Ancient Burgage belonging to John Dale', at some point in time, a John Scarrott had either shared or taken over the property. The shop appears to have been a draper's where a local man had taken a rebel soldier to buy a cap. As most of the army had already marched out of town en route for Leek and Derby, the man dared to snatch the soldier's dirk (dagger), stab him in the thigh and make good his escape by dashing through the Angel premises next door.

Chestergate early 20th century. On the left: Old Savings Bank premises, formerly 'an Ancient Burgage belonging to John Dale'; then a house on the corner at the time of the Jacobite 'invasion' where a soldier was stabbed, and further along Chestergate, adjacent to the house and shop, was The Sun Inn, originally known as The Old Bull's Head, to distinguish it from The Bull's Head (Market Place today).
This photograph is reproduced by kind permission of Cheshire Record Office.

Unfortunately some of the rebels returned to seek revenge and took two hostages: the landlord of the Angel and 'the master of the house adjoining the shop where the act was committed'. From the latter we can assume that either Mr. Burgess or Mr. Scarrott was the hapless one. Both hostages eventually returned unharmed. Sadly the same thing could not be said for Sampson Salt. He was also taken along with the Jacobites, but managed to escape and tried to contact the King's forces. Half out of his mind, he was eventually picked up near Stone and tried to tell his story. After detaining him for a couple of days, and thinking him irrational, he was turned out of their camp and hurried home.

On reaching Derby, Bonnie Prince Charlie was forced to bow to pressure from his commanders to retreat, having forced his troops to march at too great a pace. Sampson Salt had just arrived home in Macclesfield when 'the alarm was given the Rebells were coming thither

again, upon w(hi)ch he sunk down and died instantly'.

The return was a very hurried affair with the Prince marching rapidly past his old quarters. Many Jacobites robbed and pillaged; they were so short of shoes that it was reported whilst one soldier lifted up a passer-by, another soldier grabbed the shoes off his feet. Many of the ancestral homes in the countryside were robbed, but fortunately there were few reports of casualties.

The King's Forces, soon arrived and the Duke of Cumberland, finding John Stafford's house to his liking stayed three days in order to rest his troops. He was a great disciplinarian, but greatly admired and respected by his forces. The Duke and his army left Macclesfield on Friday 13th December, heading north, and eventually defeated the Young Pretender at the battle of Culloden, 16th April, 1746.

Mill Lane Property

Happily the New Year of 1995 brought a new lease of life to a very old property in Mill Lane. The derelict building (99-101) was purchased early in 1994 by a young man intent on sympathetic restoration, who also sought my help in the important choice of a name. Subsequent research revealed many interesting details well worth the subject of an article.

Restoration work in Mill Lane during the summer of 1995. This building is now excellently conserved and has been adapted for use as six luxury flats.

On 8th August 1825 the plot of land was described as originally part of a cottage garden adjoining the Wheat Sheaf Public House. At that time the Wheat Sheaf was the only pub on Mill Green; the Three Crowns was not built until the early 1830s.

The land extended backwards to include property 'fronting Lord St.', but it is difficult to deduce when this property or the larger building on Mill Lane were actually built. They had been acquired or built for Thomas Bullock with the intention of providing an independent income for one of his daughters, Mary, at the time of his death.

Thomas and his family lived with his father, Rev. Thomas in Byron's Cottage, Byron's Lane, Sutton. He was a book keeper and great benefactor, investing in property and the silk trade.

The Mill Lane property was divided internally into three separate irregular units. The trustees were John Hooley and Joseph Corbishley and an 1825 *Macclesfield Directory* reveals Bullock & Hooley as being silk men and manufacturers of Lord St.; John Hooley, Mill Lane Silk twister; Joseph Corbishley, Mill Lane Silk Manufacturer and James Gee (mentioned in the deeds as a

tenant), Butcher at No. 45 Shambles, with his residence at Sutton.

It seems reasonable, therefore, to suppose the premises were initially used for silk trade purposes, with Hooley, Corbishley and Gee sharing the larger building. During recent internal demolition bobbins were found beneath floor boards and a large brick archway with a pulley device was uncovered.

By 1831 James Corbishley had died, followed three years later by Jonathan Hooley and about that time the Lord St. property became two dwellings and Mill Lane one i.e. three dwellings under the one roof. In 1834 Thomas, still a silk man, had moved his business to St. George's St. and although the Sutton cotton mills were in decline at that period, his business prospered. By 1850 he and William Bullock (? brother) were silk throwsters in St. George's St. Mills and he owned an 'eating house' on Byrons St.

Fortunately the Silk Heritage Centre holds a box of miscellaneous invoices and letters relating to Thomas Bullock and his son-in-law. This valuable source of information helps bring to life a man and his family during the second quarter of the 19th century.

Dozen of receipts from 1830 onwards show bales of silk to London by canal, conveyed by Robins Mills & Co. The freight from Macclesfield to Manchester was handled by the J.P. Swanwick Co. which transported skips, boxes and bags of waste. However, by 1854 the St. George's St. Mills were in the hands of Richard E. Hine purchased by mortgage from Bullock.

The sale of the silk mills marks the start of a partnership with a builder called Barton, the probable father-in-law of his daughter Rachel. They acquired large plots of land e.g. Hatton St., Brown St. etc. and shared the Ground Rents. (Presumably this is how the name Barton St. came about). Previously it has been incorrectly assumed that Thomas was building garret houses for his employees, but it was purely land speculation.

Thomas had married wife, Olive, at Prestbury in 1805, during the Napoleonic wars and they celebrated their Jubilee Wedding Day' on 19th November 1855. His father, Rev. Thomas died in 1850 leaving very little estate and Thomas and his family lived on in Byron's Cottage.

He had several children baptised at Christ Church, but Thomas was one of the trustees instrumental in obtaining St. George's chapel for the Church of England community in and around the Mill Green area. A letter from a friend dated 6th July 1851 includes the sentence 'You have managed well to get St. George's out of Debt!'

His only son, Thomas, born 1826, was by the age of six years attending 'The Byrons House Academy' run by a Dickensian sounding character named Francis Figgins. He graduated to Macclesfield Free Grammar School and then Brasenose College, Oxford, finally becoming curate to Dr. Burnet of Bradford, who was formerly the 'excellent preacher' of St. George's. Then tragedy struck – young Thomas fell ill and died. His father received a heartrending letter from the father of William, one of the young man's pupils. William's father wished his gratitude to be known 'for the kind interest he took in my child the care he manifested toward him'. The young teacher's belongings were finally packed up and sent to Macclesfield by a colleague, except 'a small rosewood envelope case, I know he valued it greatly and I was afraid it could not be sent safely'. . . It was retained, together with the cap and gown, until Thomas was able to make another journey to Bradford.

Tragic episodes like this were very much part of everyday life at that time. No doubt Thomas consoled himself with a bottle of port from the fine selection of wines and liqueurs in his cellar (he was also fond of stout). He maintained a comparatively modest life style for, apart from silver sugar tongs and spoons, a china tea service, a musical box, one or two items of furniture and a secondhand piano. The piano was purchased from a renowned London retailer and transported to Macclesfield by canal (for which daughter, Sarah, received tuition). He kept a pony and trap and we learn from his good friend, John Ryle writing in July 1855 'I do not forget that you usually go to the seaside about this time of year.' Blackpool was a favourite destination as witnessed by a letter dated 16th July, 1849 from a Blackpool landlady, Mrs. Margaret Topping: 'The parlour one double and two single bedded rooms you had Last Summer will be at liberty on Saturday the 28th of this month when we shall be glad to receive you'.

Thomas died in 1868 having led a long and significant life. He left two oil paintings, portraits of himself and wife, Olive, to his daughter Sarah, wife of a surgeon, William Thorneycroft Hardern of Park Green. It would be nice to know that these portraits are still hanging on a wall somewhere.

The Wharf, Macclesfield Canal. Along the canal came good from as far afield as London, including Thomas Bullock's piano for which he paid £24 on 7th March 1827. The carriers were Pickford & Co. and a packing case was lent.

Grammar School

New roads can have a devastating effect on the historical layout of a town or city. Already it is difficult to remember the appearance of Chestergate and King Edward Street before the extension of Churchill Way and construction of the roundabout outside the entrance to King's School.

At the end of the 17th century a large house stood on Back Street (now King Edward St.) with a substantial area of land adjacent, enclosed by walls and fences from land on its eastern side belonging to Earl Rivers. The property belonged to a widow, Elizabeth Stanley, and would have neatly filled the gap between the premises of Inheritance Furniture, on the western side of Churchill Way, and Magnet Southerns on the eastern side. The land to the rear extended northwards to what is now the King's School premises.

On 22nd October 1695 the house, including oubuildings, stables and part of the adjoining land, was purchased by Joseph Eaton, Doctor of Physic from Nottingham and first minister of the Dissenting Chapel (now the King Edward St. Chapel), presumably as his residence. The property was sold again on 18th May 1703 to Charles Duckinfield of Over Tabley, who subsequently became a baronet. This would have been a form of investment, and after almost 33 years he, in turn, sold it to Peter Davenport on 1st May 1736 for £210.

Davenport was quite a character and from the facts I have been able to collate, appears to have been born in London (1684), joined the Dragoons in Windsor (1707) and was widowed at least twice, possibly three times, before marrying Lucy Frances Legh of Adlington Hall. By this marriage he became the brother-in-law of Charles Legh of Adlington and in 1746 the pair are listed as serving together on the Grand Jury in Chester.

However, this marriage by no means met with the approval of Lucy's father, although his granddaughter, Elizabeth, was baptised at St. Michael's in 1728. (The Davenports of Bramhall and the Legh family had intermarried before during their long histories).

Davenport had gained little promotion in the Dragoons; in 1709 he was a Quarter Master responsible for accommodation, food and equipment, by 1712 a Cornet (the lowest rank of commissioned cavalry officer in the British Army) and 1715 a Lieutenant in Colonel Dormer's Regiment of Dragoons which took action against the Jacobite disturbances of the following winter.

Davenport's arrogance and heavy-handedness made him very unpopular with the residents of Macclesfield & District, especially when he was appointed Receiver General for Cheshire responsible for the collection of Land Tax. He was knighted as a Crown servant on 8th June 1744.

Traffic waiting to enter the roundabout at the northern end of Churchill Way is queuing in what would have been part of a garden and stables belonging to the Davenport House, subsequently known as Holyrood House after the Pretender's overnight stay. The house provided excellent accommodation for the Free Grammar School and masters during the second half of the 18th century. The Grammar School (King's School) today can be seen in the background behind the trees and is therefore sited almost immediately behind where the 18th century school stood.

It seems strange, therefore, that Bonnie Prince Charlie's men would have sought out the Davenport house in December 1745, on their way south. Sir Peter was 'absent' but the Prince stayed in the house for just one night, Sunday 1st December, where a council of war was held. After dark the following evening the Prince left quietly to continue his march to Derby undetected – at least for a few hours! The details and circumstantial evidence are too complicated to enter into here but suggest that the Prince, desperate for supplies, had hoped to enlist Sir Peter's help. There is no evidence to support the idea that Davenport was a Jacobite sympathiser, quite the reverse, but what exists does suggest that someone was taking the opportunity to reap revenge on Sir Peter, by drawing the attention of Prince Charles Edward Stuart to the former Quarter Master's presence in Macclesfield.

A drawing of Macclesfield Grammar School on Back Street (King Edward Street) about 1775. Although the palisades appear to have been retained, there is no sign of the iron gates. A drawing including the gates subsequently came to light.

Peter Davenport's death in 1748 is something of a mystery. His wife, Lucy. had died before him (he had, in fact, married for at least a fourth time before his own death), so their daughter, Elizabeth, was left with Trustees and Guardians during her minority.

The lawyer, John Stafford, whose account of the Pretender's visit is well-known, lived in close proximity to the Davenport property. Amongst his various duties he was a trustee for the Grammar School and now saw an excellent opportunity. On 28th May 1748 he entered into an agreement to buy the house and land, which then included a garden acquired from Earl Rivers and an additional field of almost 2 acres called Byronfield, the latter purchased by Sir Peter in 1741. In the same year Sir Peter had also been fortunate to purchase 'Two Pews or Seats in the Parochial Chappel of Macclesfield' (St. Michael's) which could be transferred with the ownership of the property. The Contract cited 'John Stafford for and on behalf of the Governors of the Pofsefions Revenues and Goods of the Free Grammar School of King Edward the Sixth in Macclesfield'.

The old school building (see pages 22-25)

was almost 200 years old and totally inadequate for a modern 18th century grammar school. The new Headmaster and 2nd Master (Usher), the Atkinson brothers from the Lake District, had arrived in 1745 with plans for increasing both the numbers of boys attending the school and the curriculum; this newly acquired property provided ideal premises in which to carry out their plans.

The purchase price was £550 paid in two equal instalments by John Stafford during 1748. It is interesting to see the stipulations in respect of fixtures and fittings, just as today. All 'Chimney Pieces' (fireplaces), locks on doors, lead cisterns etc. were included. Permission was given for immediate possession and after the first payment of £275 on 29th September, alterations could begin. The stalls and stable furniture could then be sold together with any fireplaces from the house and, if considered desirable, also the iron gates and palisades (iron railings) at the front of the house.

The only concession requested by Peter Davenport's Administrators, which was granted, was an extension of six weeks for keeping their hay and corn in a convenient place in the out-buildings. The final payment of £275 was made on 27th December 1748 and the old school premises at the top of Bunker's Hill were sold in 1750.

At this time the Free Grammar School had income from its ownership of properties elsewhere in Macclesfield and also in Mottram (St. Andrew), Nantwich and Chester.

Water Supply

Perhaps it is because water is the first basic necessity of life that it has gone hand in hand with controversy, certainly throughout modern history, and probably well before. It has also been the inspiration behind many early engineering achievements and the idea that corporate bodies could make a profit by charging for its supply.

In the late 17th century two Macclesfield aldermen, Lunt and Booth, seized their opportunity to make a small fortune. At that time the town's water supply was mostly from two wells, one in Wellgate or Wallgate (now Backwallgate) and one at the southern end of Mill Street.

The natural drainage of the Common provided an excellent water supply from the Stone-pit well (today a site close by the Hovis building), from where Lunt and Booth piped water in lead pipes down across the River Bollin and up to the Cross in the Market Place. However, in 1681, the whole operation was commandeered by the Corporation and the pair 'compensated' accordingly!

A waterhouse was built at the Cross which directly supplied four houses only, on the corners of Jordangate, Chestergate, Mill Street and Churchyardside, by 1ins bore lead pipes (total cost £135. 1s (£135. 05). Technically the Sovereign owned the wastes and commons with their springs and streams, so permission should have been sought. The matter was legalised in 1685 when a grant was obtained from King Charles II, as a demand had arisen to extend the supply.

During the following year pipes were laid along Back Street (King Edward Street) and Dog Lane from Mill Street to Barn Street (through the entrance to the Grosvenor Centre and middle of the Indoor Market to Churchill Way respectively).

The Old Grammar School at the top of Bunker's Hill was supplied, from where the water was taken to Goose Lane (Brunswick Street).

In 1693 the Corporation negotiated for a cistern to be built at the Cross from a design by George Sorocold, the famous engineer who was later involved with the construction of the Derby Silk Mill (1712). Nothing further happened till, on 19th August 1736, the well in Wallgate used by 'Innkeepers' was conveniently reckoned to be prejudicial to health and 'stopt up' by the Corporation, thus increasing the revenue from a further expansion of the water supply.

Remains of the Market Cross said to have been bought by a farmer of Upton in 1798 for his dog's grave. Who would put their own initials on their dog's grave? Perhaps the letters were already inscribed (MWW – Macclesfield Waterworks) and matched his own initials. Could the date originally have been 1693 and, being worn, re-inscribed by him 1798? The stone was trimmed by a stone mason in 1968 to make the inscription clearer.

The year 1769 was an important one for water – the Corporation found it necessary to put the rates on a proper basis. Now payable on quarter days ie. 29th September, 25th December, 25th March and 24th June, a list was drawn up according to the value of the property supplied.

A public house valued at £30 paid £1.12s (£1.60) per annum and a dwelling house of the same value 15s (75p) and so forth, the burgesses were given a 50% discount! Various rules were laid down so no one could obtain water illegally.

It would seem that at this time the Stone-pit well was converted into the Round Fountain, which gave greater control over the collection and pressure of the water.

At various times the pipes became a matter of concern and Water Committees were appointed to deal with the situation. In October 1780 cast iron pipes of 4" diameter were considered instead of lead, but by August 1781 alder (wood) pipes had been chosen. An advert appeared in the Manchester newspaper in October 1783 for the sale of lead pipes by Macclesfield Borough.

Controversy ensued, by April 1794 the pipes were 'in very bad repair' and cast iron pipes of 3" diameter and more than half an inch thick were laid from the Market Place to the 'grid at the Bottom of Church Wallgate' instead of alder. The Water Rates were increased by 50% with subsequent replacement of the pipes to the top of Bowling Green Hill (near Hovis today).

In 1800 an Inspector of Coal Mines was appointed to ensure that the workings on the Common did not contaminate the water supply, and 1807 saw a filtering reservoir replace the Round Fountain (cost with increased supply £1,800).

By 1822 the supply was again inadequate and a new reservoir considered but the Corporation was now involved in grandiose schemes concerning the town centre and the new town hall. Not until 1837 did plans for a new reservoir – Leadbeaters – get underway, then the saga began.

Report 28th October 1837: the Water Committee had decided on the purchase of Leadbeater's field for £500 and an adjoining piece of land owned by John Browne; total expense calculated as £3,446. Permission was granted.

By February 1838 doubts were being expressed; a Mr Thorpe was of the opinion that 'the present reservoir' was sufficient, but one year later the Mayor was told by the Water Committee that the new reservoir was 'complete'. Mr Broderick of the Water Committee was awaiting a visit from the hydraulics engineer.

Part of the town, supplied with water from a private reservoir, was to be brought into the main system; this comprised tenants of Christopher Shaw Roe (Charles Roe's grandson) who lived near his house, Summer Hill on Chester Road.

On 4th May 1839 the Town Clerk asked when the money (£3,500) was needed; Mr Broderick said 'certain circumstances had to be noted'. Apparently the reservoir had filled satisfactorily but when it reached a certain height it began to lose water, however, the engineer intended to connect it to the original one and try the system for 12 months. He also recommended taking in Mr Roe's system immediately. A Committee member, Mr Gould said the Roe tenants had virtually been supplied with town's water already, as 'It is impossible to drink Mr Roe's Water'! Mr Broderick, a resident of that part of town disclaimed the 'imputation'.

In August 1839 the reservoir damage was reported as completely repaired, cost £102, but the following February saw leakage, though not through the crevices in the rocks. During the following three months the whole of the reservoir bottom was lined at a further cost of £230 with the result that when it filled up – it began to leak again! The answer was to puddle as with canals. Costs were rising, the August meeting of 1840 ended in uproar, but Leadbeater's survived and has served the town for more than a century and a half.

Leadbeater's Reservoir with the old Hovis building and chimney visible in the distance on the left of the view.

St. Alban's R.C. Church

One of Elizabeth I's closest friends and loyal subjects was Bess of Hardwick (c.1527-1608). She lived through unusual times when some of the nobility and great families, finding it difficult to adapt to the Church of England, steadfastly clung to their 'Old Faith' – the Church of Rome.

Other families were divided in their loyalties from which extraordinary situations arose; this included Bess's own family and the Belasyse family in Yorkshire. Both families gained extensive lands at the time of the Dissolution of the Monasteries. Paradoxically some of their descendants would have a profound effect on the proliferation of Roman Catholicism in England, and in particular the Macclesfield area.

Bess, widowed three times, married finally one of the wealthiest widowers at court, the Earl of Shrewsbury, and such was the strength of their Protestant faith that they were given custody of Mary Queen of Scots for 14 years – a considerable task.

Bess's youngest daughter Mary (by her second marriage) married Gilbert, son of the Earl (by his first marriage) and although the rest of the family remained Protestant, Mary reverted to the Roman Catholic faith. It has been argued that this was the result of her close contact with Mary Queen of Scots. Gilbert eventually became 7th Earl of Shrewsbury and their descendants have remained true to that faith.

The Belasyse brothers, Anthony and Richard were appointed to dissolve certain religious houses. Anthony, one of Henry VIII's chaplains, was granted many properties including the Manor of Newburgh (Newborough) in Yorkshire. He gave this manor to his nephew, William, whose wife was a staunch Roman Catholic.

By the 17th century the Belasyse family was one of the richest landowners in Yorkshire and the head of the family, Thomas, was created Lord Fauconberg of Yarm in 1627 and Viscount in 1642. His grandson of the same name, by an unusual turn of fate, married Mary, daughter of Oliver Cromwell.

As this younger Thomas had no heirs, the title and lands passed to his nephew – yet another Thomas. The mother of his nephew, Anne (Davenport) had been given the Sutton Estate near Macclesfield by her father to be included in the marriage settlement when she married Sir Rowland Belasyse. Nephew Thomas therefore inherited estates from both his father and his uncle, including Sutton; however, he quarrelled with his chaplains, went bankrupt, fled to Belgium and died in the English Benedictine Convent in Brussels during 1718, leaving his son and heir, Thomas, to 'pick up the pieces'.

Thomas married a Roman Catholic in 1726, but the priest who married them made great demands including a yearly annuity from his wife, and Fauconberg, in a rage, dismissed him.

The Fauconbergs leased from the crown 'the Old King's Mill' (Sutton corn mills) and from 1696 had undertaken to pay a yearly annuity of £5 from mill profits 'to support the Catholic Priest of Sutton'. Lady Fauconberg (widow Bridget) had a legal dispute in 1728 with the Mayor, Aldermen and Burgesses of Macclesfield who insisted that the inhabitants of the Borough use their malt mill, to the detriment of Sutton mills.

It seems possible that Bridget took on payment of the annuity of the the priest because, in spite of her husband's bankruptcy she would have been allowed to claim up to one third of the estate as dower. She caused problems for her son, Thomas (4th Viscount) resulting in the vast estates being divided between various Roman Catholic family members. Known as the 'raving Dowager' she died in 1732.

Although Fauconberg retained Sutton for his own use he lived mostly at Newborough but also had a London residence. He apostatised to the Church of England in 1734 but did maintain two chapels for his tenants in Yorkshire. (It has been wrongly recorded that he renounced his Roman Catholicism in 1760 – the year in which his wife died). His children were brought up Roman Catholics, except Henry his eldest son and heir who was given Sutton, presumably in preparation for his marriage in 1766.

The estate originally belonged to the Sutton family and, when in 1549 the Mass had been suppressed, William Sutton had evidently installed a chapel with a priest in Sutton Old Hall, where tenants could worship alongside the family. This continued until the early 18th century, but with the bankruptcy and death of the 3rd Viscount the annuity would have been suspended and the chapel closed; it is recorded that from 1716-20 Mass was heard in a hayloft at Ridge Hill Farm and other places.

Soon two Misses Orme built a house at Sutton Lane Ends which contained a large room for Roman Catholic services. This was used until the year 1792 and served by a visiting priest each month (the building was eventually demolished about 1884).

In 1767 the vicar of Prestbury in his return to the House of Lords regarding Papists in the parish, wrote 'in Sutton there is a Mass-house very near Ye Hall which belongs to Lord Fauconberg'. This related to the house at Sutton Lane Ends for the Sutton chapelry was then part of the Church of England and came under Macclesfield Parochial Chapel (St. Michael's). In fact Charles Roe's brother, James, Curate of Disley and shortly to become Prime Curate of St. Michael's, was married in Sutton Chapel to Elizabeth Harpur on 2nd January 1753. The entry was duly made in St Michael's register.

In 1767 there were 37 reputed Roman Catholics in Macclesfield and Sutton, only 13 of whom had lived locally all their lives. William Young, 65 years old was Steward to Lord Fauconberg and had lived in Sutton 30 years. Eight women were button makers. Six recent arrivals of two and a half years or less were engaged by Charles Roe for his copper company, so it would seem that they had been offered the work before they arrived. Catholic Relief Acts 1778 and 1791 made penalties less severe; numbers were slowly growing and the Macclesfield populace by this time included many Dissenters, so the atmosphere was right to establish a Mission in Macclesfield itself.

Above: Mothercare premises at the corner of Mill Street and Backwallgate – the site of the Roman Catholic Mission from 1792-181.

Below: This beautiful triptych – painted on wood and attributed to the 16th century – was used as an altar piece at Sutton Lane Ends. This valuable work of art has now been removed from St. Alban's Church for safe keeping although a copy is kept in the Lady Chapel.

The Macclesfield Mission

For almost the whole of the 18th century members of the small Roman Catholic community of Macclesfield wishing to attend Mass would have made their way to the tiny hamlet of Sutton each month for the service of a visiting priest. At last in 1792 it was possible to lease two rooms in a house situated on the site of what was originally part of the medieval crenellated house of John de Macclesfield, known locally as 'the castle'.

In 1789 Robert Blakeney, a Dublin ironmonger then merchant, died aged 62 years. Robert and his sister Elizabeth held investments in a large plot of land in Macclesfield which contained a good sized house (Rose's former shoe shop, two adjoining former houses and shops (Mothercare) on Mill St, several properties at the top of 'Back Wall Gate' (still Mothercare), a large yard, midding stead, slaughter house, brazier's shop and warehouse – all on the castle site.

Dublin was an extremely wealthy city, becoming the four largest in Europe in the 18th century. There had always been connections with Dublin, no doubt because of the considerable linen and linen thread trade through the port of Chester. The thread was used, together with horse hair, mohair and silk, in the manufacture of Macclesfield buttons. In 1663 it is recorded that James Stopford, member of a local family, was residing in Dublin.

By the late 18th century part of the 'castle' premises had come into the possession of Jonathan Willot a plumber and glazier, who died about the same time as Blakeney; Willot's son, Jonathan, was in H.M. Regiment of Royal Cheshire Militia. In 1792 the Trustees were forced to sell part of the premises to cover debts and at this time two rooms were evidently hired near the top of Backwallgate (now part of the Mothercare store) for the Roman Catholic Mission; one for the priest and one for the chapel.

By 1795 a French priest Fr. Louis Benjamin Robin had taken over and begun the first baptismal register. It is interesting to note that this contains the baptisms of Elizabeth (1796), John (1798) and Mary (1803) children of John & Elizabeth Willot (? John a possible relative or the same Jonathan).

On 24th June 1801 four Catholic laymen purchased a plot of land in Chester Rd from Thomas Grimsditch, a wealthy solicitor of Jordangate, Macclesfield. With financial help from many friends, especially those in Ireland,

a chapel foundation stone was laid in September 1810. Within a year the completed chapel was dedicated to St. Michael. The Church of England Parochial Chapel was also dedicated to St. Michael (and All Angels), which did create some confusion until the building of St. Alban's church across the other side of Chester Rd. (1839-41).

Was it just coincidence or genuine Irish nostalgia that inspired the choice of dedication, for Robert Blakeney had been baptised and brought up in the parish of St. Michael, Dublin, bordering the River Liffey in the northwest of the city?

The first resident priest did not arrive until Maundy Thursday, 17th April 1821. Fr. John Hall, educated and ordained at Ushaw would, during a remarkable lifetime, earn the tribute of 'The greatest priest in the Shrewsbury Diocese'. At first he occupied a room partitioned off from the chapel, but later built a priest's house and sacristy alongside. The house remains at No. 36 Chester Rd.; the chapel became a school, but was finally demolished in 1985 and replaced by a new parish centre.

By 1832 the plot of land on which St. Alban's now stands, (being the field in which Fr. Hall kept his pony) became available for purchase. With an initial loan and gifts Fr. Hall was able to buy the land for £600 by 1834 and launch an appeal for a new church the following year.

Correspondence suggests that the first architect under consideration was a Mr. Hadfield, with whom meetings took place at Dukinfield and Glossop, but John Talbot 16th Earl of Shrewsbury had other ideas. He had engaged a young architect, Augustus W. N. Pugin, 27 years of age, to work at his residence Alton Towers. Pugin also built for the Earl what was to be his masterpiece, St. Giles church in Cheadle Staffs.

Life had not been easy for Pugin, son of a French immigrant. His father, whilst working for the famous architect John Nash, had provided his son with excellent training. However, by the time he was 21 years old Pugin had lost a wife in childbirth and spent time in a debtor's prison. He remarried and shortly afterwards became a Roman Catholic which complemented his 'artistic sympathies'. He believed that the grandeur of the Gothic style and the spirit of Roman Catholicism were as one – hence his inspiration for church building.

Pugin was fortunate to have attracted the patronage of the Earl of Shrewsbury who,

St. Alban's. Macclesfield, view of the entrance through the west porch.

The house built by Fr. Hall adjoining (to the right of the picture) the Parish Hall, the latter built on the original site of St. Michael's Chapel.

though already contributing a substantial annual annuity to the Cheshire Fund, promised a further £50 each year if Pugin was engaged. By December 1838 Pugin's drawings had been accepted and the new church (completed and paid for by instalments as the work progressed) was registered as a place of worship on 28th June 1841.

St. Alban's is unique in two ways, firstly it is the only church undertaken by Pugin in the Diocese of Shrewsbury and secondly, because of the limited area of land available, the church had to be built north to south so that instead of the altar facing traditionally to the east, it faces south. This was a situation with which Pugin was not entirely happy, however the large window behind the high altar was installed as a gift by the Earl. The window itself is unusual, being dominated by the figure of St. Alban whereas, according to convention, it would normally portray one of the Persons of the Blessed Trinity.

Pugin's original design for the exterior of the building displays a much taller crenellated tower, with staircase tower on the southwest corner terminating in a large Chinese pinnacle. For reasons now lost in obscurity the complete design was never finished. More comprehensive details of the church, together with a set of excellent photographs are held in a file at the Silk Heritage Centre, Roe Street, Macclesfield. There is also a booklet entitled 'St. Alban's, Macclesfield' by Michael J. Ullmann*.

Fr. Hall was given the honorary degree of Doctor of Divinity by Pope Pius IX in 1852 and ceased his role of parish priest in 1857. Sadly he became blind in 1860 but remained in Macclesfield until his death on 1st October 1876.

The church was consecrated on 22nd October 1931 when the final loan had been cleared. A major scheme of restoration work was undertaken by Fr. C. Dwyer in 1982, resulting in the beautiful yet much simplified interior as we see it today.

*(The earlier history is compiled from my own researches).

Medieval Corn Mills, Macclesfield

The first mention of a corn mill in Macclesfield is in the Domesday survey of 1086, translated 'There is a mill working for the hall'. At that time it belonged to the Earl of Chester but, together with the manor of Macclesfield, soon passed into Royal possession and became known as the King's mill. This is identifiable with 'the Old King's Mill' (Sutton corn mills) leased from the Crown by the Fauconberg family (mentioned on page 48).

Above: a quern stone recently recovered from a building site in town close by the area of the coporation malt mill. Earlier querns were operated by hand but replaced 17th-18th century by the above. It is 2ft in diameter (61cm), the other stone making the pair is unfortunately missing.

Above: Nether Alderley Mill which is two mills under one roof. It displays a unique feature of Cheshire corn mills, that of having the water wheels inside the building instead of outside.

Initially there was only one water corn mill on the site, but a dispute of 1629 refers to 'certain mills called Macclesfield otherwise Magfield Mills' under a rent payable 'to His Majesty', whereby all the inhabitants 'upon the lands' of Macclesfield, Sutton, Wincle, Hurdsfield, Broken Cross or elsewhere in the 'Burrough Manor & Forrest' had to bring all their grain etc. to be ground at the mills.

At this time there were three millers, all with the Christian name John, viz: Faulkner, Newton and Barlowe. They accused a very important townsman, James Pickford, of erecting windmills or handmills etc. near to the town. He admitted erecting a handmill 'or Quern' in Wildboarclough and selling malt to the Macclesfield inhabitants. He argued, however, that his mill was four miles away from other mills and did eventually win the day – the case against him was dismissed.

Later evidence suggests two water corn mills (possibly under one roof as at Nether Alderley) by the early 17th century, no doubt due to the

steady increase in population during the Elizabethan period. The possibility of another mill ie. one of an early simple windmill construction, is suggested in the Castle Street area of today, because in the Earl of Derby leases for 1634 there is listed a house and croft with part of the 'Wyndemillfield'.

The latter was more than likely acquired by the Mayor, Aldermen & Burgesses during the difficult period of the civil wars when the Earl of Derby's possessions were sequestrated. Certainly the site appears to be approximately the same one on which the later Corporation malt mill was built, creating a legal dispute in 1728 when Lady Fauconberg insisted that it was to the detriment of the Sutton mills.

During the second half of the 18th century the waste water from the corn mills was used for industry. The first person to utilise this source was Charles Roe who, together with a partner, entered into an agreement with Thomas, Earl of Fauconberg, from 25th March 1750 to 'direct and convey waste and useless water to the silk mills in Macclesfield'.

In 1802 the 5th Viscount of Fauconberg, Henry, died leaving no son but three daughters and the Sutton estate passed to the third daughter, Elizabeth. After considerable scandal Elizabeth divorced her husband, the Duke of Norfolk and remarried Lord Lucan.

On 3rd & 4th September 1803 the Earl and Countess of Lucan sold the water rights of the Sutton mills to Michael Daintry and John Ryle and others including Charles, Richard and Samuel Wood, then on the 12th sold the water corn mill and other properties to Daintry & Ryle. At that time the water corn mill had drying kilns close by and the deed also lists millstones, 'running geer', pools, watercourses, dams, floodgates and sluices etc. and a house previously used as a bakehouse or oven.

Permission was given to alter the watercourse if necessary, but there was to be no interruption to the water supply for the corn or silk mills. Shortly after a lease of 1st May 1828, a 'silk factory' complete with steam engine 'of ten Horses power', had been built on the site by Henry and Richard Bennett, thus bringing to an end a tradition of corn grinding by the 'King's mill' recorded for at least 740 years!

The corn mills had been supplied with water from a stream flowing through the gardens and wilderness of Sutton Hall, which joined the Moss stream flowing from Danes Moss (the latter belonging to Macclesfield township). The point at which they converged is today the middle of London Road Terrace.

At that point there was a weir or paddle device creating a pool which would have filled the lower part of Sherwood Road with water (the probable stank or pool of the mediaeval period which at one time accommodated a fulling mill). From this weir the head of water, which had built up, was redirected into a man-made watercourse and conveyed (across what is now London Road) to Duke Street (today Jackson Street), from where it is immediately curved to the corner of Pitt Street with Coronation Street. There it entered the reservoir which diagonally covered an area between Pitt Street and Cross Street (W. to E.) and Coronation Street and Mill Road (S. to N.)

John Earles in his book 'The Streets

and Houses of Old Macclesfield' was therefore correct in deducing that the corn mills had been sited on the premises of what was then (1915) J&F Jackson's silk mill – the corner site of Mill Green where Cross Street meets Mill Road.

Confusion has arisen with Wood's Pool, formerly on the eastern edge of south park near the top of Hobson Street. That pool was constructed about 1810 by Charles, Richard & Samuel Wood 'for the purpose of supplying our Cotton Factories in Sutton'. It was fed from a large reservoir on the opposite side of London Road from the Moss Rose and water was also diverted from the weir (London Road Terrace).

This combined water supply flowed through a channel along the eastern boundary of the South Park to Wood's Pool. The pool was bought eventually by the N. Staff's Railway Co. on 5th July 1918 to supply water to a water tower by the side of the railway lines for the steam locomotives.

It is interesting to note that Peter P. Burdett, always meticulous, marked 'the Old King's Mill' in its exact location when surveying for the Cheshire map printed in 1777.

The Greenwood map of 1819 reveals two new mills on the Bollin, (Brunswick Steps area) presumably built to replace the Sutton mills. It also carries a mill symbol on the east bank of the Bollin, opposite the site of the former corn mills; this relates to Charles Roe's windmill on the Common, then converted to a corn mill.

Pitt Street. The frontage of the whole of the block of homes with garrets, on the right-hand half of the picture, represents the west side of the reservoir which supplied the corn mills. The mills were situated behind the house on the left but at the bottom of the hill on Mill Green.

Sutton – The Lamb Inn

History is full of colourful characters, not only local, but who are also of national repute. The unobtrusive township of Sutton provides several reminders of such people and helps keep the fascination with the past alive.

A view from Tegg's Nose Country Park looking east towards what remains of Macclesfield Forest.

Henry, son and heir of Thomas, 4th Viscount and Earl of Fauconberg, during his holidays from Eton school had on occasion stayed with school friends at Brocket Hall, the home of Sir Matthew and Lady Lamb. There he met and fell in love with the eldest daughter, Charlotte, and with his father's approval married her during the summer of 1766.

Thomas, through his grandmother's family the Davenports, owned the Sutton Estate adjoining Macclesfield and this, together with his approval, he generously gave to son Henry. The property would then have been added to Henry's possessions when negotiating his marriage settlement with Sir Matthew Lamb.

(Incidently Thomas was such an enormous man that during the early summer of 1759, when illness struck both people and horses throughout the country due to adverse weather conditions, the grooms on his Yorkshire estate were 'at a loss' to find a mare strong enough to support his considerable weight!)

Property conveyancing always takes time and on such an important issue as the transfer of the Sutton Estate, an important man was engaged – the lawyer John Stafford.

John Stafford, Clerk to the Manor and Forest of Macclesfield (1748-1754), lived and worked in Cumberland House, Jordangate. Not only was he responsible for the legality of the transfer, but he also carried out the work of an accountant checking the books of rentals and profits and ensuring that the estate was run in an efficient manner.

By 5th December 1766 the paperwork was finished and Henry, then legal owner, was delighted to discover from John Stafford's report that Sutton was proving 'to be superior in value' to either his own or his father's expectations.

Several improvements had been carried out so that the estimated rental for the year 1767 was £932. Even after deducting expenses John Stafford judged that the estate would be worth about £800 each year (today almost £100,000). Henry also owned other estates, so when their total income was added to that of Sutton and the £400 promised each year by Sir Matthew (under the terms of the marriage settlement), he was overjoyed to be able to pronounce his 'neat' annual income as £2,500 (today in excess of £¼million).

Several more improvements were proposed

by John Stafford but Henry decided to postpone them until he was sure of his finances. One suggestion was to fence in and lime an area of 18 acres on Sutton Common, however, Ralph 'Birchinough' who had a farm adjacent, made an offer to lime it, (cost £50) and John Stafford suggested that Ralph should have it rent free for 21 years 'excepting a few shillings by way of acknowledgement'.

Another area of land called 'Teaugues Nose Pasture' was also considered for letting. A note in the rentals refers to 'Pigclough in Tegs Nose' of 14 acres, so it appears that Teg (now spelt Tegg) was simply as abbreviation for Teaugue (or more than likely the family name Teague).

At present Mr Teague is a mystery. The name is possibly Irish and in the early 19th century there was a Thomas Teague who was a mining manager in S. Wales.

It is interesting to note that John Stafford refers to coal mines on the estate 'which several years ago were leased out to a Man who was not able to unwater these Mines...' (For the moment any connection between the Man and the name Teague can only be speculative.) In the event Henry was hoping that someone would take up the mining leases and left the matter in John Stafford's capable hands.

Further items of interest are: 'Fir Timber' valued at £500 to be felled in 12 years time; conversion of a house/farm. The latter was for conversion into an inn which John Stafford fully supported, but which was also postponed by Henry early in 1767 on financial grounds. It seems apparent that the conversion did eventually take place and Henry, in true Georgian tradition, would have named the inn 'The Lamb Arms' out of respect for his father-in-law. There seems little doubt that 'The Lamb' inn today is on the same plot of land as the original, but in a slightly different positon.

Had Henry foreseen the forthcoming scandals in the Lamb family perhaps he would have thought of an alternative name. His brother-in-law, who became the first Lord Melbourne, had an affair with an actress and singer of Drury Lane, whilst Melbourne's wife had several lovers, one of whom, the Prince of Wales, was father to her fourth son, George.

Henry's eldest son died so his second son William, who was a very clever boy, eventually inherited his father's title and property. Sadly William chose to marry his cousin, the delightful and beautiful Lady Caroline Lamb, whom he had adored since childhood.

Caroline became besotted with Lord Byron and wrote in her diary that he was 'Bad, mad and dangerous to know'; after a break in their relationship she again met Byron at a summer ball and hysterically smashed a glass, slashing her arms with the broken pieces.

Lord Byron was a member of the family after whom Byron Street and Byron's Lane in Sutton were named, but the public house sporting his name on Chapel Street, was probably just an inspired guess!

Even Henry's own family was not without its scandal. His youngest daughter Elizabeth had been forced into marriage with the heir to the Duke of Norfolk when she was actually in love with the 'handsome, extravagant and lazy' Richard Bingham, heir to the Earl of Lucan.

After 18 months of marriage Lucy went shopping and never returned. She went to live with Bingham and her husband sued for damages. The marriage was dissolved by Act of Parliament and Elizabeth married Bingham by special licence.

They lived happily together as Earl and Countess Lucan, producing two sons and four daughters, and subsequently inherited the Sutton Estate.

The present Lamb Inn (the former was on the left of the photo with its side to the road and the rear facing the present Inn) a reminder of the Lamb family.

Street Names

Names of streets and places etc. can provide important clues to the past but many can also mislead. Some seem perfectly obvious, for example, Park Lane was a lane (now a substantial road) which originally made its way across the middle of Macclesfield Park from east to west, and most people journeying to Chester will find themselves travelling up Chester Road.

Ancient street names can be intriguing and two of the earliest in the township of Macclesfield have stood for centuries, Chestergate and Jordangate.

The word 'gate' can be interpreted in several different ways; it suggests some form of entrance into or exit out of an enclosed city or town, yet is often substituted by 'street'. It is amusing therefore to read in 18th century property deeds the names Jordangate Street and Chestergate Street. With regard to Macclesfield I prefer to think of 'gate' as meaning 'the way leading to'.

Had we been able to stand at the original market cross close by the eastern end of Chestergate it would have been obvious that Chestergate itself was the way leading towards Chester, Millgate (now Mill St.) the way leading toward the Old King's Mill (the manorial mill) on Mill Green, while Jordangate was the way leading to the River Jordan.

Surprisingly the stretch of the River Bollin, as it flowed within the boundaries of Macclesfield was originally called Jordan and still retained this title on certain 18th century plans. The name could have originated from Jordan, Lord of Tytherington (1258-93) but technically the river would have belonged to the king and not to a particular individual or corporate body, although water rights could have been obtained for use of the river in exchange for its maintenance.

Another strong possibility is that Queen Eleanor as Lady of the Manor and Forest of Macclesfield named the river in remembrance of her stay in Acre in the Holy Land, having accompanied her husband Edward I on a Crusade during 1270-72. Certainly Macclesfield held a special place in her heart as the Parochial Chapel (now St. Michael's) was founded on her wedding anniversary, 1st. November 1278.

The area today close by the Castle Inn was originally known as Wellmouth, for it was the site of the Town's Well. The steep thoroughfare which now covers Backwallgate and Church St. was logically called Wellgate – the way to the

Jordangate, centuries old, the way down to the River Jordan.

The view down Church Street, originally Wellgate, looking towards Wellmouth of the medieval period.

well – and was accessible from either Millgate or the Root Market (now the south side of the Market Place).

By the 17th century two hundred years after John of Macclesfield had converted his premises into a crenellated mansion with impressive stone walls, the name produced an alternative, 'Wellgate or Wallgate'. It was not until the early years of the 19th century, when the hitherto sparsely occupied steep hill of the Market Place became crowded with dwellings, that Church Wallgate was adopted to differentiate it from the other already crowded half of Wallgate, which at the same time was in a way downgraded to Back Wallgate.

Today, of course Backwallgate remains as one word, but for reasons unknown, possibly with thoughts of modernisation when the street was widened, the Borough Council chose to adapt Church Wallgate to Church Street.

In certain parts of town the streets began to mushroom from 1780 onwards as the population rapidly increased. One particular area for development was lower Park Lane especially after the great auction of Macclesfield Park by Lord Cholmondeley in 1788, still remembered by one small street called Cholmondley St. (pronounced Chumley!).

Great naval victories in the West Indies during the Napoleonic Wars provided names for Nelson, Rodney and Vincent streets. Admiral Sir John Jervis defeated the Spaniards on 14h February 1797 at Cape St. Vincent largely due to Commodore Nelson's heroics with his ship *Captain*. There were celebrations throughout the nation and Jervis 'nobly earned his earldom' Earl St. Vincent. Sir George Rodney, another Commander, was successful against the French fleet particularly in the seas around Dominica, Guadaloupe and Martinique.

Apart from national heroes local families also recorded their names for posterity. Barton was a mid 19th century builder. Mr. Crompton and Mr. Brown leased land in Macclesfield Park which they presumably bought at the great auction. Whilst Brown's land remained in the area of Brown St. today, others exchanged or bought additional land. By 1811 Peter Crompton Esq., then of Manchester, owned land adjoining Park Lane and gave his name to both Peter Street and Crompton Road.

Charles Roe's son William must take credit for Roe St., Charles St. (now demolished), Catherine St. (his eldest sister's name) and

Shaw St. (his wife Hannah's maiden name) in the area surrounding his father's church Christ Church.

When William sold a piece of land to George Pearce a joiner on 20th February 1788 for the purposes of 'building upon', it was agreed that 'two new intended streets' would be called Catherine and Pearce but for some reason the spelling of the latter is now changed to Pierce. George also joined the privileged few to have two streets named after him, as did James Hobson, (the latter's running south from lower Park Lane).

Joseph Pickford of Royton, Lancs., cotton manufacturer, whose family was formerly of Macclesfield, owned and leased a substantial area of land in the southern part of the town until the late 18th century – hence Pickford Street. His father's second marriage was to a Miss Elizabeth Sunderland of Croydon, whose relative Richard Townley later assisted with a large loan. If we add a dash of royalist fervour the Pickfords are accompanied by George (III) and his wife Charlotte – all streets which were laid out during the 1790s.

Strange to relate only on the Enclosure Map published 1804, but prepared years earlier circa 1796, does Pickford Street appear as Sugar Street; and Sunderland Street as Pickford. So far there is no reference to be found on any deeds in that area to show that 'Sugar' was ever adopted, although one street did change name from Charlotte to Townley. And why the name 'Sugar'? Is this the clue to where the barrel of treacle fell off a wagon pulling up Mill St? The 'treacle' tradition is so strong I feel there is some truth in it, and that it happened in the late 18th century before the local newspaper came into being (1811). Someone at Macclesfield Corporation must have approved the name for the 1804 Enclosure Map, although Joseph Pickford would not have been amused and presumably insisted on the change of names (he was involved with cotton not sugar).

Apart from names relating to people and places, titles of buildings long demolished are often recorded on street or road name plates. The most obvious one in Macclesfield is the modern Castle Street, which refers to John of Macclesfield's crenallated mansion, constructed around 1398, and sited just a short distance away from its eastern end, on the opposite side of Mill Street.

(The few remaining stones from the porch

were finally removed in 1933, during redevelopment of the site, but can now be seen on display in the ground floor premises of the new extension to the Town Hall).

At first glance King Edward Street is an oddity; it does not record the King who almost never was, but takes its name from 'The King Edward VI Grammar School', which, from 1750, occupied a large 17th century house on the street at that time known as Back Street.

Another 17th century building, initially referred to in deeds as Clapham House, but subsequently recorded as Chatham House, stood in the vicinity of Chatham Street today. By the early 18th century the house, previously two buildings made into one, had been rebuilt, but retained one or two earlier features for interior use. This became the home of Charles Roe. It is surprising, however, that the name Chatham should have been chosen for a much later street.

Fortunately Cumberland House, part of which dates back to the period before the Duke of Cumberland's stay in December 1745, still remains together with its street. Unfortunately, what was originally a very fine thoroughfare with a delightful Victorian atmosphere, has been decimated by a large roundabout and new road system.

Many original street names have completely disappeared along with their streets, but are mentioned repeatedly by historians. Two favourites are Dog Lane and Welch Row. Whilst the location of Dog Lane is known, Welch Row

– apart from the one at Alderley Edge – remains a mystery.

Dog Lane and Chestergate ran almost parallel from the Market Place until they reached Barn Street (now in part Churchill Way) where Dog Lane terminated. There was a very large barn in the area belonging to the Pickford family (probably somewhere at the rear of the present indoor market i.e. the unloading bay for the market), which explains one name but not the other.

During researches in the City of Gloucester I discovered another Dog Lane. The earliest main trading route in Britain, well used by the Romans, was by boat from London up the River Thames to Lechlade, then to Gloucester via Akeman Street and Ermine Way. From there transportation was along the River Severn to the important port of Shrewsbury, where packhorses waited to carry goods as far afield as Chester, North Wales, Warrington, Manchester, South Yorkshire and, of course, Macclesfield.

Ideas, families and retainers also passed along these routes, and circumstantial evidence suggests early links between Gloucester and Macclesfield. It would be no surprise, therefore, to find early names adopted from Gloucester and other areas, just as in later centuries we find a profusion of Royal Oak Hotels, Victoria railway stations and Albert Squares in various towns and cities.

Another example is St. James's Square, (as in London); it was sited behind six cottages and a stable at the lower eastern side of Mill Street, with Wood Street today marking its southern side. The name commemorated a famous sea battle fought against the Dutch fleet off the coast at Orfordness. It took place on St. James's Day, 25th July 1666, when Prince Rupert soundly defeated the Dutch and prevented an invasion of the southeast coast of England.

A very early name has produced Hallefield, now boasting a Road, Crescent and Drive. At first glance it is a perplexing name, suggesting the mediaeval 'Hallelegh' with a possible German origin, but actually the answer is quite simple. The name refers to a large plot of land,

Cumberland House from Cumberland Street. This part of the property once had its own separate address on Cumberland Street.

Hallefield Road, a reminder of the area known as The Hollyfields of Queen Anne's day (deed of 1712).

originally owned by The King's School, which was leased out as part of its revenues. The 18th century name was Halleyfields, but at the time of Queen Anne's reign (1712) it is recorded as the 'Hollyfields'.

The compacted white wood of the holly tree is a favourite with wood turners, and was used to make the bases for Macclefield buttons, which were then covered with scraps of material and embroidered with mohair, silk or linen. Presumably the Hallefield area in the 17th century and earlier had been planted with holly trees, making a very profitable source of income for both the Grammar School and the lessee.

Maxfield Close records the alternative name for Macclesfield, often suggested as having been the name of the town at some time in the past. Although there are a considerable number of alternative spellings for Macclesfield over the centuries, yet Maxfield does not appear to be one of them officially. On each occasion I have seen it written (mostly 17th and 18th century) it has been used as an abbreviation for Macclesfield in exactly the same way as 'Xmas' for Christmas or Yorks. for Yorkshire etc.

Mention has already been made of individuals' names being given to two streets in close proximity i.e. the Christian name for one, and surname for the other, as in Charles Street (now demolished) and Roe Street. In this respect one particular resident had a great advantage – his name was SAMUEL STREET! This probably suggested the idea to him in the first place and encouraged others to follow suit.

Samuel, who was a merchant by trade, owned land in 'The Dams' area of the town, now in the region of the small roundabout at the lower end of Churchill Way. On the 11th June 1765 he married Mary Statham at Prestbury, and his daughter, Elizabeth was baptised in the King Edward Street chapel on 9th January 1767. Samuel Street still remains and , although considerable demolition has taken place in the area, his wife's maiden name Statham, and that of his daughter, Elizabeth have also managed to survive.

Incidentally Elizabeth Street married Rev. David Davies, a Doctor of Divinity, in 1804, but there appears to be no trace of a Davies Street resulting from the marriage settlement. (The one in Hurdsfield had no connection).

Property in Lower Mill Street and beef cattle

Edmund Swettenham of Somerford Booths died childless, and by his will (1756) and codicil of 25th August 1757, he left his large estate in the hands of Trustees. His wife was entitled to 'certain parts' of the estate, and his brother Philip's two daughters received all rents and profits from his several holdings in Chelford, Whirley, Sutton and Macclesfield. The Macclesfield property included two burgages on Mill Street, now the interesting property No. 96.

The interesting Mill Street property previously two burgages, then the Pig & Whistle public house. The adjacent window of the shop No.100 Mill Street, shown on the right of the photo, marks the frontage of an early 19th century stable which belonged to the burgage property (now No. 96 Mill Street).

The remainder of the estate descended to his great nephew, Roger Comberbach, on condition that he took the surname Swettenham. This he did, and it is surprising to see how many 18th century estates passed into the hands of cousins or distant relatives because there was no surviving son in the main family line.

In addition to the rents etc. the nieces each had to be provided with £500, either as a marriage settlement or at 21 years of age, whichever came first. £1,000 was a considerable sum for Roger Swettenham (previously Comberbach) to raise and, as happened in so many other instances, a very complicated situation arose whereby loans were obtained from wealthy individuals. In this particular case £600 was eventually borrowed from William Brocklehurst for a short period (1807-13); he was, of course, a member of the famous 'silk family'.

Meanwhile the property had passed from the Swettenham family to Samuel Higginbotham, a grocer, whose daughter, Elizabeth, married

James Pearson. The two houses on Mill Street, which were leased to tenants, became part of the marriage settlement and so passed to the Pearson family of silk manufacturers as an investment property.

By 1812 one of the houses remained, but the other had been converted into a bay of buildings with a stable alongside. The property also held an entitlement to two seats or pews in the Parochial Chapel (now St. Michael's) together with privileges such as grazing animals on the Common and peat from the 'Moss Rooms' (now Danes Moss) for fuel. One year later the stable had been replaced by a shop/dwelling-house.

From 1834 the whole property passed through several hands because of deaths, loans and two remarriages of a widow, until finally on 28th September, 1867 the owner was Thomas Frost, a gentleman of Manchester. By then the pre-mises along Mill Street had been converted into a public house called the Pig and Whistle with a dwelling-house. The landlord, who would remain there for several years, was John Clegg.

The ground floor of the pub was (and still is) built into the hill side at the rear and therefore on a level with the graves from the adjoining Quaker graveyard, in fact, one, relating to a character called 'Martha,' is just through the wall!

Behind the pub, built on a series of terraces, was also a cottage, brewhouse and slaughterhouse, and John Clegg at his own expense had to 'sufficiently uphold, cleanse, whitewash, paint and maintain' all these properties which were now part of the complex.

On 9th November 1878 an amusing incident tool place whereby a solicitor, acting on behalf of the Trustees of the Friends Meeting House, wrote to the Brewer's Manager, Thomas Thorp of Charles Street, Stockport, to point out that a spout or gutter, for carrying water from the pub roof, rested on the burial ground for a distance of 28 feet. Also woodwork of an outhouse had been placed in the burial ground wall, and these encroachments, made by the former owners of the Pig & Whistle, would have to be removed.

It is interesting to note that these encroachments had not been taken up with the previous owners. Perhaps the Trustees appreciated that Thomas Thorp might lend a more sympathetic ear. The only remaining grave outside the former Quaker Meeting House happens to relate to members of a Thorp family, whose patriach was Samuel, buried in 1860 aged 69 years. Is this just coincidence or could there have been a family relationship?

In 1919 the Pig & Whistle was given its present day black and white mock Elizabethan facade, but then sold by auction at the Angel Hotel on 24th July 1921. The premises contained an 'Entrance Hall, Bar, Bar Parlour, Smoke Room Snug, Music Room, Kitchen, Outside Washhouse, W.C. Yard, three Cellars, large Clubroom and three Bedrooms'. The frontage was 38 feet in length, The accompanying dwelling-house subsequently became a butcher's shop at No. 98 Mill Street, but this has now ceased to exist, having become part of the larger premises at No. 100 Mill Street.

The public house underwent further conversion, resulting in the premises of R. Marshall Carr Ltd. as seen today 'retailers of Chandeliers, Hearth & Door Furniture, Dog Grates & Fire Baskets etc.

An excellent engraving dated 13th December 1811 by W. Robinson of a beef shorthorn, bred by Robert Colling of Brampton near Darlington, reproduced by kind permission of Alderley Village Butchers, Alderley Edge. Some time ago the present proprietor worked for a family of butchers near Manchester who were direct descendants of Robert Colling.

This beast would have been typical of the type of cattle dealt with in the slaughterhouse to the rear of the premises of what are now Nos. 96 and 100 Mill Street. The British Isles led the world in developing cattle for beef. The Colling family successfully bred from the dual-purpose shorthorn (milk and beef) to produce exceptional beef cattle, hence the engraving. The present owner of R. Marshall Carr Ltd. recalls the remains of a building with a stone floor, into which was secured a large iron ring for tethering each animal in turn for slaughter. This building was set back, behind the site of the former butcher's shop (the latter previously the stable).

Jordangate

The answer to the question of where the name 'Jordangate' came from is well worth consideration; it has previously been attributed to Jordan of Macclesfield.

Now part of the Market Place, but until the 19th century this block of properties was the start of Jordangate.

Today there are very few streets or ways remaining with the suffix 'gate'. There would not be many originally, partly because of the small population in the early mediaeval period and the way in which it was scattered throughout the country. Even perusing plans of the larger cities, such as London, York, Chester etc. it is very unusual to find a 'gate' prefixed with the name of a particular individual. The favourites, of course, are East, North, South and West.

There is the occasional saint e.g. St. John, or reference to a particular holder of an office, as in Bishopsgate, London and Deansgate, Manchester. An exception is Billingsgate, but even that is attributed to a king of the Britons called Belin. Jordan, therefore, seems an unlikely choice at that time, as it referred only to a local resident.

Generally, in the first instance, evidence does seem to suggest that a gate or entrance existed, and the way leading to it adopted the name as a logical indicator of the direction in which to go.

A Macclesfield property deed of 1335 refers to half an acre of land lying 'outside the gate which leads to Tytherington'. Another deed of 1401 indicates land adjacent to 'ye Highway

leading to Tytherington' and by the reign of Philip and Mary (1553-1558) this highway was known as 'the King's or Queen's road'.

At this early period, as this route was largely unadopted, there was no necessity to give it a particular name, however, by the 19th century, when dwellings began to appear along its fringes, it became Beach Lane, the spelling altered to Beech about 1850.

Until the creation of the name Beach Lane, circumstantial evidence suggests that Jordangate, which ran from the corner of Chestergate, extended part way along the lane at its northern end, to the gate leading down to the river and towards Tytherington.

Very early records from 1329 refer to a Pyrlewall Meadow, which was located approximately in the area of Pearl Street today. So could the gate have been in the wall which marked the northern limit of Jordangate in line with either Pearl or Coare Street, and even Northgate Avenue? Certainly the drop of the hill, from what is now King Edward Street, would have been much gentler originally, levelling out in the vicinity of Pearl Street.

Old Hall Street relates to the southern boundary of an area of land known as 'the Old Hall field' (deed 1825).

In the 1820s, John Brocklehurst, who lived in Pear Tree House (now Jordangate House) and owned a large area of adjacent land to the north and east, began to develop and sell, with the result that the lower half of Hibel Road, leading down to the River Bollin, became Cockshead Lane. Whether or not this was a corruption of Cockshoot is not known, but it does correspond with the name of a farm in Bollington called Cockshoot Hey Farm which, about the same period, became Cockshead Hey Farm!

By 1842, John Hibel, 'a Spirit Dealer', owned a substantial amount of property in town, some of which he had purchased from the Earl of Derby, and about this time Cockshead Lane became Hibel Road. (Incidentally the 1841 directory incorrectly records it as 'Cockshut').

Unfortunately some early deeds, which have been transcribed in later centuries, can no longer be found, so there is no way of checking the spelling of names. Jordanesgate very rarely appears, but in documentation where it is found, the name Jordaingate far outnumbers the former. It seems to have been the historian, Ormerod, in the early 19th century, who first suggested that Jordangate was the way leading to Jordan of Macclesfield's house, but the property in question (deed 1375) is translated as land and grange: at that early date a grange was a barn for storing corn not a residence.

Jordan of Macclesfield's house might have been somewhere within the borough boundary, although it could have been in the vicinity of the Cumberland House site today, as his father was Queen Eleanor's forest bailiff. (The area at that time would have been in the forest limits).

If the Jordan in Jordangate does not relate directly to an individual, then it must relate to the river. On 25th April 1552 the 'Free Grammar School of King Edward the Sixth in Macclesfield' came into being, although it was actually a refounding of the school after the religious and political turmoils of Henry VIII's reign. The school needed a reliable source of income to ensure survival, and benefactors generously gave property from which rents and other income could be obtained. There were many perils ahead, particularly because of the affiliation between the school and the Parochial Chapel (St. Michael's). The 17th century was a difficult period with many people having to take court action to prove ownership of property. The Jacobite rebellions of the early 18th century again caused uncertainty, so it was imperative for the property deeds to be kept safe and secure. The grammar school was no exception and ensured that an official copy of all its holdings was legally put together. These were compiled in book form comprising carefully executed plans.

On three of these plans the River Bollin is clearly shown as the River Jordan i.e. that part flowing along the stretch which today is from the bottom of Brook Street to Hibel Road and Beech Lane, at which point it curves from a westerly to a northerly direction. These plans were obviously copied from very early deeds, and as the earliest mention of the Bollin occurs

Hibel Road – view from the footbridge showing the turning to the left into Beech Lane. Jordangate extended across the foreground of this picture before the installation of traffic lights and the new upper section of Hibel Road.

about 1400, it is likely to have had its own local name before that date.

The name Jordan was obviously brought back to Europe at the time of the Crusades and certainly occurs in Saxony at that early period. If Queen Eleanor felt inspired enough to persuade her husband to go on a Crusade to Acre, encourage the building of what was intended to be the largest Cistercian Abbey in Europe at Vale Royal, and personally promote a chapel for Macclesfield, then it is not beyond the bounds of possibility that she named the river, flowing beneath her chapel, as Jordan.

Christmas 19th century style

Georgian Christmases are barely discernible amongst the diaries, books and notes of the period. However, with the incredible swell of population during and after the Napoleonic Wars, the last three-quarters of the 19th century saw Christmas grow in significance, as the commercial potential was appreciated more and more.

Readers of the *Macclesfield Courier and Herald* were kept informed of Festive reports, as in the instance of Christmas 1834, when Queen Victoria's uncle, William IV was on the throne. An article read, 'The Liverpool market was never better stored than it was on Christmas Eve'. One steamer from Ireland had arrived with 'no less than fifteen tons of plucked geese' on board, which had sold from eighteen (old) pence to three shillings apiece, by today's values in the region of £6 to £12 each. Apart from the geese it was estimated that there were at least eight thousand turkeys also for sale in the market.

At this time a correspondent near Doncaster kept the local paper informed of interesting articles relating to that area, such as the one which appeared in the *Doncaster Gazette* with the surprising headline 'GREEN PEAS at CHRISTMAS' –

'On Christmas Day, the table of Mr. Donor of Skirlaugh was furnished with a beautiful sample of green peas, and the whole were equal to any grown in the summer. What is remarkable, the garden is somewhat exposed, being newly laid out, and the quickset hedge not more than one foot high'!

By the mid-Victorian era, the quaint droll reporting, which was a hangover from the Georgian Period, had long passed and journalists were beginning to realise that tragedy, gloom and crime, were making far more impact and encouraging sales of newspapers. What better evidence than the articles appearing in the *Macclesfield Courier and Herald* edition of 2nd January 1875?

'The calamitous Christmas of 1874 will be a date long remembered'. One such catastrophe was received by way of a brief telegram from Madeira dated Christmas Day, which informed that the emigrant ship *Cospatrick*, bound for Auckland from London, had been totally destroyed by fire the previous 17th November, whilst off the coast of South Africa. All hands were lost, apart from three survivors found adrift, with the total fatalities reckoned as '470 souls'.

That Christmas had experienced very severe weather conditions with many reports of deaths in the snow. The Registrar General was moved to write on the subject of how cold affects mortality and, using several statistics, deduced that 'mortality from cold increased 8 per cent for every year of age, or it doubled every nine years from the age of 10, as it did in 1855'. His advice was: 'The cold is most effectively combated by exercise, which excites the heating energy of the system, and warmth is sustained by nutritious food, by artificial heat, by warm woollen or fur clothing . . .'

We are led to believe that the judicial system of the past was severe, often to the extreme, yet, with regard to Macclesfield I have found a good deal of leniency shown on several occasions. As always, whatever the century and

Adverts which appeared in the *Illustrated London News* on 19th December 1891.

crime, and wherever it took place, the outcome depended on individual attitudes, as the following examples demonstrate. (There are those, of course, who will argue that 'Good Will Towards Men' was very much in evidence, as it was Christmastide).

The first local incident (still Christmas 1874) relates to three young boys who set alight a corn stack in a field off Daybrook Street, Hurdsfield with matches 'which they got from a bakehouse'. The property affected belonged to William and George Foden, timber merchants of Beech Lane. The damage was estimated at £7 or £8. Mr. George Foden said that the field was 'very often trespassed upon', but seeing the boys were so very young he did not want to press the case.

The newspaper was also full of incidents involving drunkenness and assaults arising from the festivities. The same thing happpened a year later when James Green, a silk dyer, was charged with being drunk and disorderly in Green Street, and for assaulting a policeman. This seemed to be typical of a 'policeman's lot' at

Engraving entitled 'Decorating the Pulpit' from the *Illustrated London News* 26th December 1891.

that period and was accepted by all as part and parcel of the job! 'The defendant (James Green) was drunk and so riotous that he throttled the constable', who somehow managed to get assistance in moving Green to the lockups.

When the case was brought before the Magistrate, Mr. Bullock, he decided that in view of it being Christmas time and Green having been locked up since Saturday (it was now Monday), if Green promised not to offend again he would be dismissed. There was a chorus of 'hear hears' from those of the public who regularly attended court proceedings. The Defendant said, 'I'll promise not to come here again'. Mr. Bullock responded, 'Then you'll be a good lad, will you?' Defendant, 'Yes'. Mr. Bullock, 'Get off with you, then'.

Concerts abounded, particularly in church and chapel halls, and the Drill Hall was very popular. An amusing write-up concerned the Macclesfield Choral Society, whose members practised throughout the Christmas period for their annual January concert which always took place in the Drill Hall. On 31st January 1876 it

was reported that a performance of 'The Messiah' was to take place, for which Mr. Seal, the conductor, 'has for many weeks past been drilling the members'! I hope he enjoyed the pun.

A week earlier a 'Grand Military Concert' had taken place in the Drill Hall by the 'renowned band of her Majesty's Grenadier Guards', the opening overture was 'William Tell'.

The weeks before Christmas 1875 had seen S & W Berisford, 44 and 46 Mill Street advertising 'Wines! Wines! Wines! A Great Variety of Sherries Pale Gold & Brown from 18/- to 120/- per dozen (the cheaper bottles retailing at about the same price as a smaller Irish goose). The very pale dinner sherry was recommended at 27/- per dozen and a choice of vintage ports, brandies and 1870 clarets were advertised together with 'Old Skotch – Irish whiskies, Nicholson's gin' etc.

For superior advertising and superb illustrations, however, Macclesfield readers would have had to turn to the *Illustrated London News*, as shown by the above photographs.

New Year stories

What a startling revelation! New Year readers of the Macclesfield Courier, 1895, learnt that there were three North Poles, as verified by Dr.S.C. Chandler. Firstly the magnetic pole, where the needle dips down vertically, said to be at $70\frac{1}{4}°$ in the extreme north of Canada. Secondly the geodetic pole, lying at the northern end of the earth's shortest diameter and thirdly, the pole of rotation, which everyone thought was the same as the geodetic pole until someone discovered that it varies from year to year.

The bitter winters of the period encouraged an enthusiasm for skating. J. Halstead Cutts, 32 Mill Street, had 300 pairs of skates for sale. Not to be outdone Lilie & Day, 39 Mill Street, offered skates by the best Sheffield Manufacturers and were the sole agents for 'Douglas' skates considered 'the best in the world'. The choice was surprising and as varied as today's trainers viz: 'Club Beezer, Forbe's, Acme, Windsor, Caledonian' etc.

J.R.Isherwood 'BOTTOM of MILL ST.' had a good stock of boots guaranteed durable and waterproof, and just in case anyone was in doubt, Daniel Oliver of 15 Hope Street West, Macclesfield, had written the following on 6th November 1894 – 'Dear Sir, It is just three years last Wakes since I first visited your shop to buy a pair of boots. I bought a pair that I thought would suit me and I have only had them half-heeled since. I have stood in water for hours when I have been fishing up to the shoe-tops but I have never been wet-footed yet. I was so pleased after twelve month's wear that I bought my son a pair, and although he has worn them every day for two years, he has never had them mended yet. Wishing you to put thish letter before the public . . .'

Hovis Bread, as supplied 'to H.M. The Queen and Members of the Royal Family' was being advertised as a cure for indigestion – no doubt appropriate after the New Year festivities!

Four years earlier (Christmas 1891) had seen an announcement of the marriage to take place between Princess Victoria Mary, only daughter of the Duke and Duchess of Teck (allowed the titles Prince and Princess by the King of Bavaria) to the Duke of Clarence. The young Duke died of pneumonia shortly before the wedding, and Princess Mary subsequently married his younger brother who became George V.

Both Queen Mary and her mother were great promoters of the British Silk Trade, in fact the Duchess of Teck visited Macclesfield on Tuesday, 16th April 1895. There was great excitement in the town and Alderman Pickford presented an address, 'Macclesfield is particularly indebted to Your Royal Highness for the generous disinterested (sic) and sustained efforts you have been pleased to make on behalf of the British Silk Industry'.

The Corporation had elected to spend £80 on decorating public buildings, but with the Borough Surveyor in charge, who did not intend 'to spoil the ship for pen'orth of tar', a further £50 was granted.

Lunch took place at the Town Hall with the Royal table in the shape of a horseshoe. The inner edge was outlined with a beautiful selection of arum lilies and other choice plants, placed on a silk foundation. In the hollow of the horseshoe were arranged palms and 'other exotics'.

There was only time for the Royal party to visit one silk mill, that of Messrs. Birchenhough & Sons, Park Lane, from where the Duchess walked across the roadway, beneath a rich canopy and along a scarlet cloth laid specially for the occasion, to the School of Art. She opened an exhibition, the most interesting item of which concerned J. Hall of Lord Street, Macclesfield, who, for many years, had been experimenting with rearing silk worms and, despite the vagaries of the Macclesfield climate, had had some success.

A Royal Supplement was enclosed with the local paper on Saturday 20th April, which included an interesting item regarding Queen Victoria. As a young girl of 14 years of age she had been visiting several 'great Houses' with her mother, the Duchess of Kent. They had been staying with the Marquis of Westminster at Eaton Hall near Chester and on 19th October 1832 were enroute to Chatsworth House in

The Old Year helping in the New. *Illustrated London News* 1st January 1881, 'Let us close the year with gratitude for the blessings we have enjoyed, and, amid all existing troubles, let us exercise a faith in the future, which will enable us to wish one another a Happy New Year'.

Derbyshire. After lunching at The George, Knutsford, it was found convenient to change horses in Macclesfield. Huge crowds lined the streets as the four carriages of the Royal party pulled into the Macclesfield Arms Hotel shortly after 2 p.m. The Duchess and her daughter did not alight, and a little while later, complete with a team of fresh horses, the carriage was escorted to the Cheshire boundary by the Macclesfield Troop of Yeomanry as they made their way towards Buxton.

Queen Victoria always gave New Year gifts to the poor. The New Year Edition of the *Illustrated London News* for 1891 gave notice that beef and coals were to be presented to the poor of the parishes of New Windsor, Holy Trinity and Clewer the following Saturday, and that Her Majesty would make her usual donation to the Royal Clothing Club at Windsor.

A review of the year 1880 has one or two familiar 'rings' to it. It had been one of moderate sunshine and fairly good harvests, in fact, Ireland 'happily, has reaped crops more abundant and splendid than has fallen to her lot for many years past'. There had been violent thunder storms in many places, but flooding was due to 'new methods of draining, combined with defective appliances for the storage of water, than to the caprice of Nature'.

'We are learning our lesson somewhat slowly, it must be confessed, but we ARE learning . . .'

The political news was also familiar, 'Parties have changed their positions . . . they who were in power and who, no doubt, expected to remain so for some time to come, ventured to appear to the constituent bodies and were beaten' (Gladstone replaced Beaconsfield).

A great catastrophe at this time was the subsidence of the Cheshire salt mines. An area of 50 acres known as Platt's Hill rock salt mine had been completely submerged and could never be worked again. Another 'great chasm' had opened up across a road way leading to Messrs. N. Ashton & Sons with such a roar, that it was heard for miles around. Fears were expressed that the subsidence would continue and possibly reach Fletcher's, considered to be the largest salt mine in the world, which extended beneath a crowded area of Northwich.

Opposite: Christmas 1891, Princess Victoria Mary of Teck. As Queen Mary she purchased a pair of oak candlesticks from Arighi Bianchi & Co, which were supplied to Sandringham Palace for £2 9s. (£2.45p.) Some years later she ordered a matching pair, by which time the cost was £4 9s. Together with George V she gave two large pewter incense burners to the town, which, for many years, were on display in the former Brocklehurst (now West Park) Museum.

Burials in Macclesfield

Behind the premises Nos. 50 to 54 Mill Street lies one of Macclesfield's intriguing mysteries. An early 19th century deed contains an undated and separate plan which clearly indicates a burial ground with a slightly curving boundary, set some way back behind the Mill Street premises. The 1871 O.S. map unfortunately shows a reduced length and more regular shape because of subsequent building on site.

Queen Victoria Street. The stone retaining wall on the left shields what remains of an old burial ground.

Ignoring the laying out of Queen Victoria Street and the construction of the large stone retaining wall on the western side, the land would have originally continued sloping down towards the River Bollin in a more undulating manner. This area, in fact all the land to the east of Mill Street, was probably designated as part of the Manor and Forest of Macclesfield at the time when the borough was created in the early 13th century; certainly early deeds suggest this.

The area to the east of the Market Place, where the Parish Church of St. Michael's now stands, must also have been Manor and Forest, otherwise Queen Eleanor would have made provision in some way to the Borough at the founding of the original chapel in 1278. This is further emphasised by the fact that in John de Macclesfield's 14th century deeds for two 'underground taverns' (today the cellars from 35 Market Place to 5 Mill Street), he paid a rent to the Lord of the Manor.

There is no disputing that a narrower form of the present Church Street was originally Le Wallgate (Wellgate), and extended further south with what appears to be a bend in it. A deed of 1360 refers to property lying in the

street called Le Wallgate', and subsequent ownership suggests that it was also part of the Manor and Forest. This property was subdivided by 1395 and the deed refers to four parcels of land lying to the west of the property 'as far as the boundary stones'. My interpretation is that the boundary stones were somewhere along the eastern side of Mill Street and approximately opposite the Castle Street area today.

After the completion of the Parochial Chapel in 1278 burials took place within it, and subsequent graveyards can readily be traced: so how old is the burial ground (or what remains of it)

50-54 Mill Street. The Sale notice of 17th December 1891 makes interesting reading. No. 54 was a shop and dwellinghouse occupied by the Imperial Tea Co. Two rooms over an archway linking it to No. 52 had been leased to No. 52, which was the public house The Horse and Jockey. The pub premises comprised a bar, snug, taproom and parlour with a yard and stabling at the rear. Earlier in the century a garden had occupied the yard. Also included were, of course, the two rooms over the archway. No. 50 was the site of a dwellinghouse, shop and printing offices belonging to Messrs. Brown & Son, printers and stationers.

adjacent to Queen Victoria Street?

Because the undated plan had been married up to the earliest deed of 1821 in the deed packet, I had erroneously assumed that the graveyard was very early and only discovered when building and gardening work had taken place at that time. Therefore when originally writing this article, I speculated that there could have been a connection with a leper hospital and burial ground, giving the following details:

In the Eyre roll of 1259 there is mention of protection needed for the warden of the leper hospital at Macclesfield. At that time people were forcing leper hospitals out of towns and cities to more remote areas, so could this be why the warden needed protection, because evidently he was under threat of some kind?

Only two years later Prince Edward, later to become Edward I and husband to Queen Eleanor, confirmed the rights and privileges of the Borough which had originally been granted by Ranulf Blunderville, 6th Norman Earl of Chester and Lord of the Manor of Macclesfield.

Many of the burgesses would have lived outside the small village in the surrounding environs, but were probably anxious to extend their premises in and around the area of Chestergate and Dog Lane (site of the present day Indoor Market). Their business was to trade and they would be concerned with the establishment of a good market and warehousing facilities close by within their burgages. If later centuries are an indication, they would send a son, or another member of the family, together with servants, to reside in these premises which they would visit from time to time. These burgage properties eventually became the town houses of wealthier families, whilst others leased or bought parts of them for their residences.

As more burgage plots were taken up within the Borough to make up the permitted 120, it seems likely that they extended down the western side of Mill Street. Because of the fresh water supply from the important well in Wallgate at Wellmouth one would expect the leper hospital to have been nearby but out of Borough limits. However, it is easy to imagine the desire of the burgesses for an unimpeded water supply and for the removal of the lepers.

Until 1278 the more important local residents would have been buried at Prestbury Church, but where were the poorer ones buried? There has been reference in the past to a chapel of St. Mary presumed to be in Macclesfield. A document of 1240-1257 reserved rent to the chapel. However, it is interesting to note that in 1214, when the Cistercian monks moved to Leek in order to establish Dieulacres Abbey, they occupied the site where there had been a chapel dedicated to the Blessed Virgin Mary. Later Macclesfield deeds, relating to a property on Chestergate, show a rental payable to the abbot of Dieulacres Abbey, this is surely a continuation of the same source of income from one to the other at the Leek estate. It is possible that some of the small community of monks had moved into the fringes of the forest near Macclesfield in order to take care of the lepers.

In John de Macclesfield's deeds there is reference to 'capella nova', translated as 'new chapel'. This could suggest the existence of an old one which had served the burial ground and been incorporated into his 'castle' during the building process; but now this idea seems unlikely. It is difficult to speculate without definite proof, and as my daughter points out 'capella' is Latin for a she-goat. Not so strange as it first appears, for in the 17th century, when the Earl of Derby was in possession of the old 'castle' premises, part of the land was 'the Goat field' of 6 acres. Perhaps this was what John de Macclesfield had acquired and the witnesses had met there, as was legal tradition at that time, to witness the establishment of his claim to ownership.

NB. One year after this original article (1998) due to a plan for a proposed garage on the Mill St. site the County Archaeologist, Adrian Tindall, kindly supplied me with further details:

In July 1840 the churchwardens of St. Michael's purchased a piece of land, described as 'in Back Wallgate', from a Mr. Sargent for a proposed burial ground. But the ground proved unsuitable, so on 28th May 1852 as Act was passed allowing the site to be sold and the corpses removed to 'some other similar place of interment within Macclesfield'. Exactly what happened next is not known. but it is strange that the site was purchased in the first place when Christopher Shaw Roe, grandson of the famous Charles, had given an extra area of land to enlarge the Christ Church graveyard in 1832.

Until the building of the Parochial Chapel in Macclesfield (founded 1278) the more influential families of the area would have been buried in Prestbury Church, with the poorer ones buried elsewhere.

From 1278 local burials took place within the Parochial Chapel, which was dedicated to All Hallows, or alternatively All Saints (the site of this today would approximately cover the southwest quarter of St. Michael's Parish Church).

One of the earliest burials must have been that of Thomas of Macclesfield, (circa 1302/3)

An unusual gravestone lying near the west or main door of St. Michael's.

Part of the graveyard outside St. Michael's parish church. Prior to 1686 burials took place inside the chapel, parts of which are now incorporated into the present building.

bailiff of Queen Eleanor, although according to his will he had been preceded by his son – (translated from the Latin) 'And my body to be entombed in the chapel of Macclesfield, where I attended, before the Altar of the Blessed Virgin . . . where my son Richard lies'.

According to an historian (Coulter 1938) Thomas was buried with his horse, as was his son, Jordan, which the historian found to be 'unusual'. This historian finds the interpretation unusual and unfortunately misleading. The Latin of Thomas's will is written with many abbreviations, which would have been well understood at that period. The sentence in question, literally translated, reads 'And heart body my best horse my respected overseer (? deputy forest bailiff). All wills were of similar form so it is easy to deduce that after the burial of Thomas's heart and body, he wanted his best horse to be given to his overseer, no doubt someone who had served him well.

The best horse was usually given to the local priest who would perform the burial service, but in this instance he received a very lavish gift of gold vestments.

Poorer families were also buried inside the chapel but their graves were used over and over again. When sufficient time had elapsed, a grave would be opened up, the bones and skull removed and stored in the charnel-house, and a new occupant given the space. The charnel-house, which could have been a vault, was more-than-likely situated at the eastern end of the Macclesfield chapel, for when extensions were made to the Parish Room in 1977 many bones were discovered beneath the ground but allowed to rest in peace.

Beneath the Savage Chapel, built circa 1504 by Thomas Savage (who was Archbishop of York and buried shortly afterwards in York Minster), there is also a graveyard. A deed dated 26th September 1808, regarding a sale of property in the Root Market on the south side of the Market Place, specifies one notable exception in the sale, 'the Chapel called Earl River's Chapel adjoining the Parochial Chapel of Macclesfield and the Cemetery or Burial Ground under the same . . .' (In 1639 Viscount Savage had married the daughter of Earl Rivers and by special grant was allowed the title of his father-in-law.)

By 1686 it was impossible to accommodate further bodies within the chapel itself unless, of course, the family already had a vault, so permission was sought to begin burials outside the building. Unfortunately the Grant by licence, and other original documentation, is now lost, but a Victorian Borough Council official (?Town Clerk) quoted from the licence, then in his possession, when replying to an enquiry from a member of the public regarding the consecration of burial grounds.

Old documents were once again in Latin and the licence referred to an enclosure around the chapel 'conveniently contiguous' and staked out as part of the 'ortia' (from hortus = garden) which was taken to mean old school or church garden – furthehr proof that the original Grammar School was for a short period accommodated in the Savage Chapel. However, the transcription could be in doubt and the Latin word meant to be 'actus' , which indicates a right of way for driving cattle through. As mentioned in an earlier article I suspect that cattle were kept in an enclosure at the top of the 108 steps awaiting slaughter (today the greater part of Sparrow Park), so either is possible.

Whatever the word, the area of land is not in doubt and burials continued around the outside of the chapel, until in the late 18th century once again 'saturation point' was reached. A myth has been perpetuated that in some way the water supply became contaminated by decomposition of the bodies. There is no evidence for this assumption, the water supply was piped to the Market Place from the Common via (what is today) Brook Street, Waters and Church Street, then across the Market Place to the cistern at the Market Cross close by the eastern end of Chestergate. Seepage into the water supply, therefore, does not seem possible.

The story has probably arisen from an illuminating letter written by the Prime Curate of St. Michael's, Rev. Thomas Hewson, to the Bishop of Chester on 19th November, 1775, in which he points out 'it is now very Difficult to find any place in the Chapel Yard where a Corpse can be buried'. So difficult was it to find a space that bodies were buried barely a foot below ground. After quoting further distressing details he concluded that this may be the Cause of some Pestilential Disorder amongst us', which appears to have inspired the deduction of a contaminated water supply!

This letter marks yet another turning point in the story of burials in Macclesfield.

Before taking leave of the Parish Church two particular gravestones are of interest, in fact it would be more accurate to say three. The first is a large one immediately outside the main doors of the church inscribed James Roe (brother of the famous Charles) and Prime Curate of St. Michael's from 1756 to 1765, but James already has a gravestone tucked away behind the Savage Chapel. The assumption must be that with building extensions and re-arrangement of the stones, someone thought his had been lost and went to the expense of having another one made.

The second oddity (see photo) was pointed out by a reader. How did the remains of such an important personage as a son of the Earl of Moray come to grace the pathway leading into St. Michael's? Very much by default.

As the present Earl of Moray points out, the inscription is incorrect in virtually every respect; he can find no trace of a George (Stuart) on the family tree. Intriguingly the burial entry in St. Michael's register has been altered to read 39 years at date of death, not 50, occupation 'Painter' (?artist)!

I have traced a Lt. Col. George Stewart who dashed into the Glenmalure Valley Co. Wicklow, June 1800 during the rebellion, but missed capturing the notorious rebel, Dwyer. (Roe & Co. were at this time mining in the Wicklow Mountains, Ireland and had their own private army volunteers). Army lists show a George Charles Stewart appointed Lieutenant (not Lt. Col.) on 20th April 1814, 88th Regt. (1st. Battalion The Connaught Rangers), on Irish half pay from 25th May 1816. Had he accompanied returning personnel to Macclesfield hoping to make his fortune by claiming aristocratic ancestry? This was so typical of the Regency period.

The complex issue of late 18th century burials in Macclesfield cannot be fully dealt with in one article, and rightly belongs to the Charles Roe story. However, a brief mention must be made to complete the progression from mediaeval burial ground to public cemetery in Prestbury Road.

Macclesfield, as elsewhere, began to experience a population increase not, as erroneously put forward in the past, because people were leaving the land and rushing into towns, but because many more children survived childhood (for various reasons), became adults and reproduced. The increase was everywhere, both in town and country, resulting in dramatic changes by the turn of the century.

It seems inevitable that the larger a thing becomes, the more the cracks appear, and human nature being what it is ensures that in an expanding population factions seem unavoidable. Rev. Hewson, the new minister of St. Michael's, created a crisis but, as already mentioned he also inherited one regarding burials. His assistant curate Rev. David Simpson, brought to Macclesfield by Charles Roe (June 1772), chose not to emphasise High Church rituals. By nature he was an excellent preacher, detested by a few but applauded by many; he became the 'thorn' in Hewson's side.

Charles Roe strove to remedy the situation, but at every turn he was confronted by Hewson's stubbornness and spite. However Charles saw an excellent opportunity to alleviate the situation. In his lower field, behind his Chestergate home and near the Dams Brook, was an area called 'The Marled Bank', aptly named because of its clay content – ideal for burials! His offer was a generous one: by deeds 20th & 21st July 1773 he, 'at the instance (sic.)' of St. Michael's churchwardens agreed to 'vest in and convey to the Mayor, Aldermen & Burgesses' of Macclesfield an area 70yds by 80yds from what is today the corner of Bridge Street and Great King Street.

This was regarded temporarily as an extension of St. Michael's graveyard so, surprisingly, a few early burials are entered in St. Michael's register as though they were buried there when, in fact, they were in the Christ Church burial ground.

Today the area covers (east to west) from the wall on Bridge Street to almost the middle of

The greater part of the original graveyard, now on the north side of Christ Church, conveyed to Macclesfield Corporation by Charles Roe in July 1773. The church, constructed on Charles Roe's private land, was not actually built until 1775-76.

the Corporation car park and, (north to south) from the wall on Great King Street to (including) the very first row of gravestones on the north side of Christ Church.

A quarter of the ground area, which now lies nearest Great King Street, was given free for pauper burials, but the rest was to be purchased from Charles Roe. It would have been an enormous sum for the Corporation to find, so Charles was allowed to sell each grave for not more that two guineas, as reimbursement. In his inimitable public spirited way he sold them for one and a half guineas (a saving to the purchaser by today's values of almost £60).

The land was staked out, graves dug in neat rows, lined with bricks and whitewashed, suggesting an easy task for a team of miners. Hewson claimed exclusive right of burial, which Charles had never legally consented to. Politics took over resulting in the building of Christ Church on Charles Roe's private land adjacent to the burial ground in 1775/76.

Shortly after this various amendments were made to the Toleration Act of 1688, giving additional rights to Dissenters and eventually Roman Catholics, so that after the Napoleonic Wars some chapels developed their own small burial grounds. On 23rd June 1832 a deed stated that several cemeteries 'of several churches in the Parochial Chapelry of Macclesfield were insufficient for the internment of corpses', so Christopher Shaw Roe (grandson of Charles) gave to Christ Church 'a certain piece or parcel of ground adjoining the Old Cemetery' towards the west, containing 3,240 square yds (approx. 90 x 36), which today runs along Catherine Street and is partly occupied by the other half of the car park: half of this additional land, including the latter, was specifically for pauper burials.

Another Macclesfield myth can now be laid to rest. It concerns a gentleman called William Sparrow, said to have fallen to his death whilst working on the Christ Church tower. His gravestone has been preserved close by the church, and tragically reveals that his three and a half year old daughter was buried at the same time as himself. This is a remarkable coincidence, particularly when remembering Rev. Hewson's mention of a 'Pestilential Disorder' creeping through the town. Further investigation in St. Michael's registers has revealed that William Sparrow was far from being a builder's mason, in fact he was an apothecary (chemist)

Gravestone close by Christ Church which has given rise to a popular myth.

and the symbols on his gravestone are those of a Freemason!

By 1855 the 'Burials Question' had become a national concern and the Privy Council, meeting at The Court of Buckingham Palace decreed that burials were to be discontinued in St. Michael's church and churchyard 'excepting in now existing vaults and brick graves, wherein each coffin shall be separately entombed in an airtight manner' or family graves which could be opened to a depth of 5 feet without exposure of remains.

Only one body was to be allowed burial in other graveyards where the grave was new i.e. had not been opened previously; these were Christ Church, St. George, St. Peter, in the burial grounds of the Primitive Methodist Chapel (Park Lane), St. Alban's Roman Catholic Chapel, Roe Street Chapel, Park Street Chapel, Brunswick (Wesleyan Methodist) Chapel, Bethel (Baptist) Chapel and Towneley Street Chapel and also in Trinity Churchyard (Hurdsfield).

The time had arrived for the establishment of a Burial Board by the Corporation to consider the problem of providing a public cemetery for the Borough. On 8th May 1856 the Mayor and 16 others met and decided to advertise in the Macclesfield Courier and Staffordshire Sentinel for tenders to be put forward, offering eligible sites of land limited to 50 statute acres 'for such a purpose' – and yet another saga was about to begin.

On May 15th 1856, the Macclesfield Burial Board Committee reported the findings of their inspection of the Higher Beech Estate in Tytherington for the site of the proposed Public Cemetery. It was found to be advantageous in every way, including subsoil and drainage, and Mr. Bullock (mayor) was requested to purchase the land on behalf of the Committee.

Two weeks later, however, a letter was received from the Governors of the Macclesfield Free Grammar School stating that they were offering part of their property near Westbrooke, but were negotiating with Mr. J. Brocklehurst M.P. to add his land to theirs in the offer. Two other tenders were also received.

By July 3rd, nine other offers had been made, including the one from the Grammar School, which now made four sites available viz: (to nearest acre) Upton, 38 acres (£250 per acre); Whalley Heyes, 18 acres (£300 per acre); Park Side, 39 acres (£200 per acre) and Chester Road, 9 acres (£200 per acre). A surveyor then undertook to examine the sites.

Monthly meetings continued with very little progress until October 1857, when the Clerk was instructed to offer the Grammar School £4,000 for the land in Upton, comprising 25 acres 3 roods and one perch.

By November 5th, for some reason, the offer was increased to 27 acres 2 roods and 24 perches @ £160 per statute acre and the Committee agreed to purchase, instructing the Clerk to advise the Secretary of State.

At this point, one of those amusing episodes took place. A Mr. Smith had purchased several trees and shrubs for the anticipated cemetery. The Committee refused to accept them, politely informing Mr. Smith that he must move them temporarily into the Park (West) at his own expense, and then remove them from there at his pleasure!

By December 17th, the Board had written to the Secretary of State deferring purchase. Evidently something was happening behind the scenes, and on March 4th, 1858, Mr. Bullock was asked to see the Governors of the Grammar School to find out 'Upon what terms the Land in Upton can be purchased'. Almost two months later, the 27 acres 2 roods and 24 perches were agreed @ £160 per acre.

Following this, incredibly, the next meeting did not take place for two and a half years! Finally, by way of advertisement on March 21st 1861, 20 guineas were offered as a prize for the best design and lay out of the land.

January 1862 saw approval for the design by the Macclesfield architect James Stevens. A further advert 14 months later requested plans for three chapels, Church of England, Dissenter and Roman Catholic. Once again, Stevens won first prize of £15, a firm from Darlington was second, prize £10, while one from Derby won the third prize of £5.

The plans were formally accepted at the October meeting, providing capacity for 100 persons each in the C of E and Dissenting chapels – both with spires – and 60 persons in the Roman Catholic chapel – no spire but a bell turret.

£3,500 was borrowed from the Public Works Loan for these buildings, but on March 24th 1864, the Roman Catholic priest asked permission to begin burials in that part of the cemetery allocated to Roman Catholics before the chapel's completion, due to 'the danger attending the burials in their Chapel Yard'. (No hint of what 'the danger' was is provided.)

The Bishop of Chester consecrated the C of E portion on May 17th 1864.

In 1866, the Town Clerk was instructed to take proceedings against anyone infringing or-

The former C. of E. chapel in the public cemetery, Prestbury Road. The Roman Catholic chapel was demolished some years ago and the Dissenting chapel is now part of the crematorium.

ders relating to burials in other graveyards. The first to be found 'wanting' were the Minister and Wardens of Christ Church, where a mini revolt had taken place. They considered it quite wrong to deny people burial when they already owned family graves in their churchyard, however, it was discovered that one or two new ones had been made since the regulations had been put in place.

Totally undaunted, a special deputation set out from Christ Church and saw the Home Secretary in London, stating that they had been misled by the Town Clerk. They requested continuation of burials for widows in husbands' graves etc. but the Town Clerk held firm, denying that he had ever suggested that such burials could continue at Christ Church.

So vigilant was the Corporation, that soon other culprits were recorded. The Rev. Field of Hurdsfield expressed his regret, as he had been ignorant of the orders, and gave a profuse apology for his burials, so proceedings were withdrawn.

On June 30th 1867, the Surveyor reported the burial of a child at St. George's and a report of the circumstances was called for. Burials were still possible at St.Paul's, for the Rev. Henry Briant submitted a report that two graves had been opened up but 'contained water which had to be carried out before burial could take place'. (This, presumably, related to new graves already purchased, but not previously used, before the regulations were altered).

The architect, James Stevens, on March 14th 1867 was given instructions to prepare a plan for an Entrance Lodge and gates on Prestbury Road, estimate £400 (which inevitably was exceeded).

Finally in November 1868, the entrance gates were fixed in place and the work was almost finished. It had taken from May 1856 to November 1868 for the Burial Board Committee to almost complete its task. Ironically, the final item of expenditure, which was approved in January 1869, was an amount of £2 for bulbs to complete the borders!

The cemetery lodge and entrance gates completed 1868, architect James Stevens of Macclesfield. By a strange quirk of fate the first 15 members of the Dormel Choir met and rehearsed in the lodge during 1947. The choir, renamed Mydel, is shortly celebrating its 50th year.

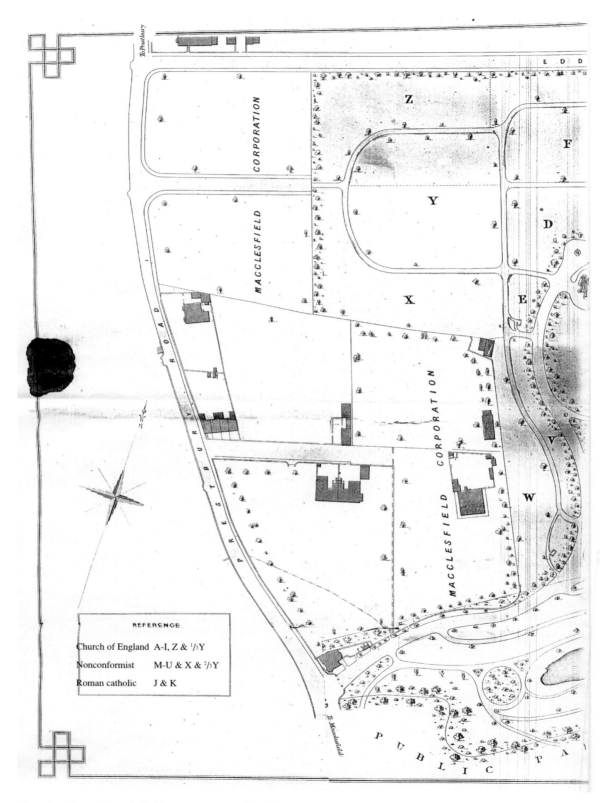

Victorian plan of Macclesfield Cemetery reproduced courtesy of Macclesfield Borough Council.

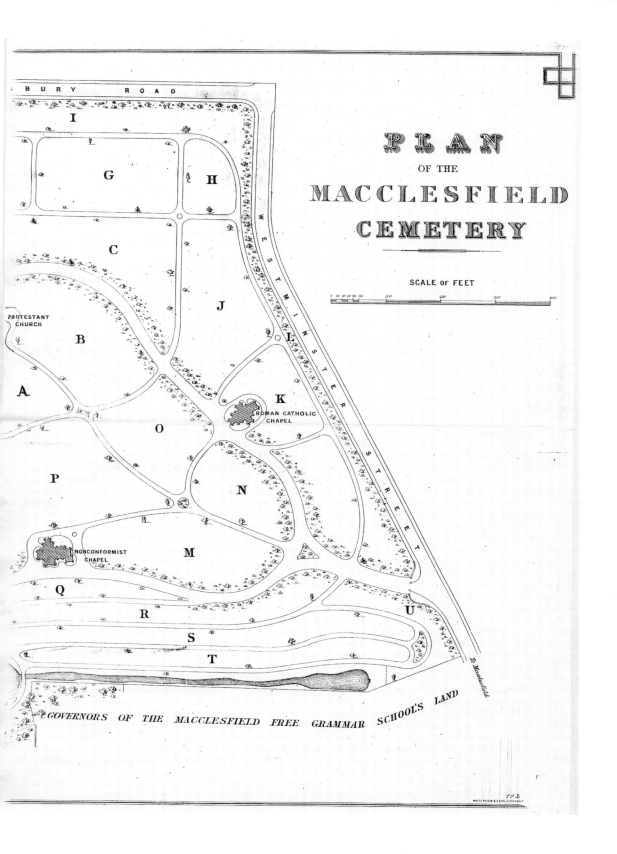

PLAN
OF THE
MACCLESFIELD
CEMETERY

SCALE OF FEET

BURY ROAD

PROTESTANT
CHURCH

WESTMINSTER STREET

ROMAN CATHOLIC
CHAPEL

NONCONFORMIST
CHAPEL

To Macclesfield

GOVERNORS OF THE MACCLESFIELD FREE GRAMMAR SCHOOL'S LAND

The Dormel Singers

Dorothy Mellor, (d. September 1983) a not inconsequential singer turned music teacher, once commented to a national newspaper that Macclesfield was not a musical town. This was the comment of an indefatigable character, with an overriding passion and zeal for music, who considered that even second best had to be treated with a temporary tolerance in her never-ending quest to be first past the post. The evidence can be found in her creation of a female choir 'The Dormel Singers'.

Adlington Hall visited by Handel in 1741 and 1751. The Hunting Lodge was an appropriate venue for celebrating the 40th Anniversary of the Mydel (Dormel) Ladies Choir on Saturday 10th October 1987 with a Dinner Dance.

Dorothy's comment on Macclesfield was a little harsh, as history can prove.

The first official establishment of music in the town would have come from the founding of the Parochial Chapel (today represented by St. Michael's Parish Church) in 1278 by Queen Eleanor of Castile, wife of Edward I. At the burial of each secular priest it was usual for others to sing, chant and pray during the night of the funeral, for which the priest provided money in his will. The first recorded instance of this in Macclesfield was in 1536 when William Bridges, priest and schoolmaster, asked for 30 priests to sing and pray at his funeral. Some probably made the long trek from Manchester where, by the early 15th century, a college or community of secular priests had been established; the forerunner of Manchester Cathedral and Chetham's School of Music. A will for John

Glover of Manchester (1590) records that he was 'one of the singing men in the College there'. His family name would later become synonymous with silk and Macclesfield.

To this day the choristers of St. Michael's are privileged to wear cassocks of red, the royal colour, in memory of the royal foundation.

William Bridges, obviously fond of music, appears to have encouraged his pupils to sing. To each who could, he left 2 pence; the others a penny. After the refounding of the school on 25th April 1552 close by the chapel, the boys would have formed the choir for Evening Prayer. Today The King's School still maintains a strong musical tradition, established over 400 years ago.

The next great musical influence in the town came from the Legh family of Adlington Hall, whose passion for music inspired the construction of a uniquely positioned organ in the Great Hall. Built circa 1670 and tentatively attributed to Bernard Smith, the organ stands on a balcony supported on either side by a huge oak tree! The 18th century saw a vibrant Charles Legh in possession of the estate; he acquired a copious collection of poems, hymns, anthems etc. and his sister, Elizabeth, a patron and ardent admirer of Handel, was an excellent harpsichord player.

On two occasions Handel visited the Hall; firstly on his way to Dublin in the autumn of 1741 (where his first public performance of the Messiah took place in the spring of 1742); secondly in 1751, when he set 'A Hunting Song' to music, written by Charles Legh. By this later visit the Leghs had completed a grand ballroom and there is little doubt that many local eminent townsmen and their families, including Charles Roe, were invited there to meet the maestro.

Charles Roe's passion for Handel's music ensured that singers from as far afield as Oldham, Liverpool, Manchester and other parts of Lancashire made up the choruses for performances of the Messiah and Judas Maccabaeus at his New Church (now Christ Church). The seed was sown and in 1933 the Macclesfield Music Festival was developed from the Christ Church Festival.

Over the years Macclesfield has gained a reputation for producing excellent choirs.

'Born' in the Cemetery Lodge in 1947, where early rehearsals took place, (Dorothy Mellor's husband James was the Cemetery Superintendent) the Dormel choir faced stiff competition, for Macclesfield already supported the very successful J.L. Riley Festival Choir (now Oriana). Dorothy's ambitions saw fruition as her choir gained many honours over the next few years, not only in Macclesfield but elsewhere. One of the greatest triumphs was in 1950 at the Llandudno Festival when the Lord Mostyn Cup was won after beating the ladies section of their local rivals by just 4 points!

In October 1952 they followed the future Orianas into broadcasting and built up a repertoire mainly of British composers, as preferred by the B.B.C. at that time.

In 1971 Dorothy retired due to ill health and the choir voted to continue, taking the name 'Mydel' from Mydelfield mentioned in a deed of 1400, which appropriately would have been somewhere in the vicinity of the cemetery.

When writing for a 10th Anniversary publi-

cation in 1957 Dorothy expressed a desire to perform the 'Messiah' with assistance from the Male Voice Choir, this she achieved shortly afterwards. Although Handel's popularity in general has never diminished, it can be of no greater significance than here in Macclesfield.

Hazel Grove 1949 – first festival success for the Dormel Singers – The Worsley Harrop Memorial Cup.

Dorothy Mellor receiving the Bullthorn Rose Bowl at the Macclesfield Music Festival, October 1957, on behalf of the Dormel Choir for the most artistic performance. The presenter, the Mayoress May Hooley, herself a choir member, was present at the first rehearsal. She has remained loyal for 50 years, very closely followed by Mabel Harvey of Congleton.

Hunting Lodge – Macclesfield Forest

It is always extremely difficult to view history through modern eyes. Buildings which are now literally streets apart and yet which were once very much connected (e.g. a grand house and its lodge, separated by a housing development on what was originally fertile parkland) can quickly lose identity in the rush for modernisation. Demolition and a couple of generations on, without specific documentation, are the means by which a local controversy or legend is born. With the addition of a few centuries, such has been the case with the supposed original manor house of Macclesfield, the ancestor of our modern town hall.

The five breeds of hounds used for hunting to the 13th and 14th centuries – as depicted in an old french manuscript.

The first important point to remember is that the sovereign was Lord of the Manor and Forest of Macclesfield for a very considerable period i.e. from about the time of the Norman Conquest until 1936 (except for comparatively short periods when it was given in dower to consorts, or during the Commonwealth Period of the 17th century). Occasionally it was leased out, but that does not mean that the manor house was included in the contract.

The initial survey of 1086 records one mill to supply 'the Hall', held by Robert Fitzhugh, together with 12 acres. This was certainly not a grand castle in the Norman style and later records are very clear in referring to the castles of Chester, Flint, Rhuddlan (Ruthelan), Beeston etc. but Macclesfield and Overton always come under the title of 'Manors'.

Even so one would be forgiven for expecting a royal manor house to be a grandiose affair, but English monarchs like many of their subjects, have found themselves short of revenues from

time to time, with the resultant curtailing of expenses. Also other considerations must be taken into account.

The royal household was constantly on the move, which gave subjects the opportunity to see their monarch and petition for favours. The giving of alms was an important part of these peregrinations from which many people benefitted. Because of the large entourage it was important for the household to make only short stays at each abode, partly because of expenses (sometimes they stayed at an abbey or manor house where the occupants could find their resources quickly depleting) and partly because of hygiene (it was always necessary to scrub out premises after each visit).

The most important royal visits, from the Macclesfield point of view, were during the reigns of Edward I and his great grandson, Edward of Woodstock, Prince of Wales, known simply as 'The Black Prince' by the Victorians. The first visit of Edward I to Macclesfield was

24-26th August 1275. In all he made 6 visits, on one occasion staying only overnight, but returning a week later; all visits were less than a week long but part of a hunting itinerary, suggesting that 'the Hall' was used very much in the capacity of a hunting lodge.

Edward's father, Henry III, when visiting Chester, for fear of contracting the plague, preferred to stay in a city of tents permanently retained beneath the castle walls. The royal family was well equipped for travelling and Edward was always accompanied by packhorses and carts. In 1279 it is recorded that he had three long carts for the wardrobe (clothing, bedding, drapes etc. and items relating to the peformance of official duties e.g. small tables, quills, parchments etc.). The pantry, buttery and kitchen each had one long and one short cart, these doubled as tables and one as the royal bed, particularly when camping out in the open. The king's silver plate and robes, together with furnishings for the royal chapel, were carried by packhorses, which numbered 41 in 1279.

Edward I, therefore, had no need for an elaborate residence in Macclesfield manor, in fact, after Queen Eleanor's death in 1290 (the manor had been held by her in dower from the time of their marriage) he never again visited the area. The manor reverted to Edward, who remarried to a 7 year old French princess, Margaret, in 1299, a political marriage which was not successful; he died in 1307.

However, 5 years earlier, in 1302 the Chamberlain's accounts record work carried out in the manor. In addition to work on the manorial buildings monies were paid for 'repairing the enclosure of Macclesfield park broken in many places by the wind storm within the present year'. No reference is made (as in other instances) to a wooden fence, carpenters or timbers, and as the park covered a considerable area, the ideal type of enclosure would have been an earthen bank topped by thick hedging.

The most favoured species for this type of hedging was 'Quickthorn', or hawthorn, which achieves a height of 12-15ft (average about 4 meters) and provides an extremely dense and thorny growth, able to withstand quite strong winds.

There is, however, a specific reference to 'repairing defects in the fence 'del Coumbe' of Macclesfield and this area is readily identifiable from a 17th century plan in the Earl of Derby collection.

The area of the 'Combes' extended a little to the east of Shutlingsloe hill, but on its western side covered the whole area west to Sutton Common, where was situated Blackcombe's Gate, the entrance to the Combes. On the north side the White Combes stretched in a narrow strip to include the present Tegg's Nose Country Park. A pack of hounds was kept and trained in the Combes ready for the Black Prince's visits, and on 2nd March 1355 he ordered a proper enclosure of the area, which he understood could be done cheaply.

Somewhere between the Combes and the parkland stood the Great Hall, but where was the site and what supporting evidence remains today?

viewed from Tegg's Nose country park; the area of the Combes hunted by the Black Prince, from Shutlingsloe in the west (in the background on the left of the photograph) to the boundary of Sutton Common in the east.

From Guild Hall to Town Hall

Some time after Queen Eleanor's death in 1290 Macclesfield Manor was leased to John Burgoillon who was reimbursed 6s. 10 pence and a farthing (34p) in 1302 for repairs to certain houses, timber and nails bought for the great hall, and nails used in mending the roof of the great chamber. Carpenters were engaged for the work and also men to whitewash the walls of the hall.

Sutton Hall today. I believe this to be the site of the original 'Hall' mentioned in the Domesday Survey, later particularly used by Edward I, Queen Eleanor and their great grandson The Black Prince, when hunting in Macclesfield Forest and holding court sessions.

One year later timber was felled and prepared for repairing the barrier around the manor together with the stable wall. A considerable amount of work was done to the stable, the roof was thatched, walls plastered and new boards and nails bought for repairing windows and 'lattis' work.

Another important job for the carpenters was to cut 27 logs into planks for repairing the manor bridge and to complete other repairs to it.

Six millstones were bought for three mills and wages paid for 'mending the ponds and wears of the said mills'. This suggests an in-creasing population attracted to the area because of Macclesfield Borough with its burgesses and their families. The complex of mills and ponds ran south along the western side of Cross Street from Mill Green, to eventually traverse what is now London Road, to a pool or stank at the bottom of today's Sherwood Road. However, it seems possible that the early mill mentioned in the Domesday Survey was nearer the Hall.

At this time John de Sutton, forester, was responsible for the area 'del Coumbes' and also the parkland where he paid workmen for mow-

The original carriageway to Sutton Hall and the farm. The stone bridge is a replacement of 1863 but the original wooden structure would have been the manorial bridge, leading south to the Blackcombes. The Rossendale brook flows beneath the bridge and enters the River Bollin in the area known as 'The Wilderness' in the background of the photo.

retained Macclesfield Manor, for in 1347 her grandson, the Black Prince, persuaded her to exchange it for two of his manors in Wiltshire and Dorset.

Apparently the manorial buildings had been neglected, for immediately the exchange took place the whole of the great stable was repaired, also the Queen's hall (great hall) and chamber and the King's great chamber, with all of them enclosed by an earthen wall.

In 1351 the Justiciar of Cheshire advised the Black Prince to dispense with his grandmother's officials in the manor and the Hallmote court (court of the lord of the manor) which would be held in the King's or great chamber, because he (the Justiciar) would hold eyres there instead i.e. he would visit periodically with his officials and hold a court session as part of his circuit.

The plague arrived in 1353 during which it is estimated that half the population of Macclesfield died, inspiring the Black Prince to pay his first visit in October of that year. The following year the manorial pond, meadow and orchard were enclosed, and a fence constructed around the meadow and pond.

At this time, therefore, the manorial buildings comprised the great hall; the King's chamber, from where many directives, written by the Justiciar and his officials, were sent to various parts of the country by royal command; the Queen's chamber (Eleanor of Castile's probable bedchamber) and the great stable. The stud had been dispersed in 1348 but was re-established in 1354 when four mares (in-foal) were bought.

On 6th July 1355 it was reported that the great hall had been unroofed by the wind, but could be repaired year by year to save costs. Accepting this the Black Prince evidently rejected its use for further court sessions, as he shortly paid $1/2$ mark to hire a similar hall. On 15th August 1357 his officials recommended him to make a new hall 'at the town of Macclesfield' in which to hold the eyre. The old hall, obviously weakened, was probably also inconveniently situated for holding court, otherwise the original site would have been used.

The Black Prince died before his father, and his son became Richard II in 1377. During the 1390s John of Macclesfield, one of Richard's favoured court officials, was busy creating his crenellated mansion in town (later known as the Castle). There was a strong religious connection between the Macclesfield and Sutton families and I suspect that John of Macclesfield

ing grass and putting up hay into cocks for the stud and deer. He appears to have lived to a great age and leased a large area of land from the Black Prince which, when it passed to his grandson, John, was 100 acres (presume Cheshire which equals just over 212 statute acres).

The area, therefore, was under the Sutton jurisdiction suggesting the adopted name. At the time of the grandfather's death (1362) Sutton Manor did not exist. The Chamberlain's accounts for 1357-1374 show Sutton as a demesne township under the Lordship of Macclesfield Manor. By the time of the grandson's death (1411) the manor called Sutton existed and he owned it; so what had happened in between times?

Edward II's reign started well with his child bride Isabella, but his mother still held her dower lands, which were finally appropriated for Isabella and must have included Macclesfield Manor. After the Queen dowager's death Isabella's subsequent concern with politics and her adulterous affair with Mortimer caused a national crisis, but still a question mark remains over her involvement in her husband's murder of 1327. By 1330, stripped of her lands, she 'retired' yet must have persuaded the sovereign to give the redundant hall to John de Sutton, at the same time creating Sutton manor. The corn mills were supplied with water from a feeder stream which began in the 'Wilderness and Garden' of what became Sutton Hall, at the confluence of the Bollin and Rossendale Brook and ran west in the direction of today's Sherwood Road area. (see page 53). The mills and manorial buildings of Macclesfield Manor had always been part of the same complex, thus the great hall would have been on the site of Sutton Hall.

On 26th August 1815 the Countess of Lucan advertised Sutton Hall for leasing together with 'a Spacious garden, Pleasure Ground and Shrubberies, double Coach House, excellent Stables and other Outbuildings. A tenant may be accommodated with about twelve acres of land'. Could this have been Robert Fitzhugh's twelve acres recorded in the Domesday Survey of 1086?

Having considered the site of the original 'Hall' of Macclesfield Manor, it is now time to move into the township in order to continue the story of the guild or town hall.

The first bid for independence by the influential families in the Macclesfield area is said to have taken place about 1220, when the Lordship was leased from the Crown by Ranulf Blunderville, Earl of Chester. There is no doubt that the Crown retained the power, but Blunderville must have obtained permission to grant local heads of families the right to establish a merchant guild, because Macclesfield by this period had a well organised market and fairs. In all probability the reason for giving such a grant was its position along one of the main salt routes into Derbyshire.

Eventually the merchants could afford to purchase a royal charter in 1261, by which they became burgesses, each committed to leasing a burgage plot of one acre at twelve (old) pence per annum within well defined limits from part of Chestergate south, known as the borough. Privileges were granted but although the burgesses were exempt from paying tax on goods, the salt tax remained and was reserved for the Earl of Chester as Lord of the Manor, who by this time was the son of Henry III, soon to become Edward I. An unusual arrangement pertained whereby Edward's wife, Eleanor of Castile, held the Manor and Forest as part of the marriage settlement, but the borough affairs were evidently kept with the Crown.

Adaptation of a drawing said to be the Elizabethan Guild Hall of Macclesfield, at the corner of Churchside and the Market Place (i.e. on the southwest corner of the present town hall site). It was 'modernised' in 1678 when the stairs were completed together with 'other outward works'.

The Burgesses now obtained some judicial power, whereas previously they had operated as a form of medieval Chamber of Commerce. They could not be sued or judged outside the borough except in the case of serious crimes for which they were tried at Chester. At this time there was no mayor but the charter did give provision – 'They may choose their leader themselves provided that We or our bailiff give counsel or consent'. It seems obvious that even the bailiff would have to consult with the Crown before allowing such an appointment, however in 1330 the burgesses, using their own interpretation of the charter, grasped their opportunity and elected a mayor.

Some years earlier, probably at the time of Edward I's death in 1307, they had evidently tested authority by providing a goal for the borough, but were fined by Edward II in 1310 for their action. As previously mentioned after Edward II's murder in 1327, the Queen dowager, Isabella was stripped of her lands in 1330, but had retained Macclesfield Manor. There seems little doubt that once again the burgesses

The late 17th century Market House (or Hall) at Winster near Matlock in Derbyshire; well worth a visit as it displays many characteristics of the Macclesfield Guild Hall at that same period viz. style of windows, large upper chamber, arches giving admittance to shops etc.

saw an opportunity to further their powers by electing a leader and holding their own court, particularly as 1330 was the year in which Isabella's lover, Mortimer, was tried in London and hanged at the Elms, Tyburn on 30th November.

Yet, as previously, their actions were called into question, this time by Edward III in 1350, but as his son, the Black Prince, had now become involved in Macclesfield affairs it seems probable that it was his assurances which obtained confirmation of the office of mayor for the borough from his father.

From this time onwards the courts of the burgess assembly are recorded under the name of 'Portmoot' over which the mayor was given permission to preside, but always in the presence of the Steward of the Manor and Forest of Macclesfield who represented the Crown.

Presumably the Portmoot took place either in the mayor's house or at the old Hall. From 1355, when the Black Prince hired a hall for half a mark per annum in lieu of the storm damaged manorial hall, the Portmoot must have convened in the same chamber as the other two courts. One was specifically for the Manor and Forest whilst the other was for the Macclesfield Hundred; they were held monthly, one following the other, but the Portmoot, which dealt with the legal side of borough business (a forerunner of the Town Clerk's Department of later centuries) met every three weeks. The mayor, who was in effect the Borough Treasurer of recent times, also held 'court' to deal with market etc. affairs.

The Black Prince needing money for his French campaigns was in no mood to finance a new guildhall for Macclesfield, so when the intrigues of Robert Foxwist (a Macclesfield forester) led to the murder of an official sent to arrest him, his lands and property were seized by order of 14th September 1358 and granted to John de Cressewell, with the proviso that the houses were 'ordained to be demised elsewhere'. They were in fact demolished and reassembled in the market place for use as the court house!

This original 'Mote Hall' contained four shops by 1374 with a public chamber above. The remnants of this building survived as four shops until 2nd October 1778, could these have been owned by Thomas Mottershead as two shops in 1715 which were then repurchased by the Corporation for demolition? The Corporation as owner, ordered the demolition of the Mote Hall together with the steps at the 'South End'. The 'Gates' were removed from the entrance which was walled up, and the walls were lowered to the same height as those of St. Michael's churchyard.

Excavations to lower the level of the Market Place in 1878 revealed the jambs of the western doorway of the ancient guildhall which were said to be 'on a line with the north side of the

Mill Street. The entrance to the 'King's Gaol' which was situated for centuries behind 34 Market Place (today the Chicken Spit). The Corporation authorised the sale of the gaol house on 29th March 1822, at the same time as the original designated plot for the new town hall on the N.E. portion of Mill Street.

churchyard', and on the site formerly occupied by the remains of the old market cross. The mouldings suggested a rather ornate doorway and at that time were supposedly removed to West Park for public viewing.

It is evident that a new guildhall had been constructed at some time, most likely in the late 16th century when, with an increasing population, Elizabeth I granted a more extensive charter in 1595. The Corporation now comprised the Mayor, Aldermen and Burgesses who were allowed to meet in the guildhall to make laws governing the then borough. The hall, occupying the southwest corner site of the present town hall complex, was 'modernised' in the late 17th century. An order of 17th April 1678 reads 'that the staires of the Court House of the sayd Burrgh bee compleated and finished att the Public charges . . . (and that) other outward works as is necessary att the same Courthouse bee done in like mannerr'.

The historian Corry, describing it in 1817 noted the display of the Corporation Arms over the entrance representing a lion rampant, grasping a wheatsheaf, with the motto 'Nec virtus nec copia de sunt', which according to his information had been 'mistaken by a tippler for the sign of an ale-house'.

The 18th century saw Macclesfield rapidly develop into an opulent town. This was not an unusual case, for it was happening nation wide as the population and advances in technology increased.

In writing a pamphlet addressed to the population in the region affected by the eathquake of 16th September 1778, the Bishop of Chester pointed out 'By the flourishing State of your Trade and Manufactures, you have for many Years been advancing rapidly in Wealth and Population. Your Towns are every Day growing in Size and Splendour; many of the higher Ranks amongst you live in no fmall Degree of Opulence, their Inferiors, in Eafe and Plenty'.

The older citizens and manufacturers of Macclesfield, such as Charles Roe and John Ryle, Snr. had worked hard and economically to bring about this 'revolution', but it was the turn of the younger generation to plan a town centre worthy of the approaching new century.

One very important stimulus was that in March 1787 the Comptroller of the Post Office at last agreed to forward mail to Manchester via Macclesfield. Surprisingly until then it had always gone via Knutsford; in fact in April 1706

John Ward, a lawyer of Capesthorne Hall, had commented that Macclesfield had made little effort to obtain the postal concession for Manchester and 'there's an end of all hopes of making Macclesfield a post town'. It was an important source of remuneration and recognition.

Alterations to the market place advanced in the 1790s, as the Mayor, Aldermen and Burgesses (i.e. the Corporation) began to find ways in which to fund the operation. Water rates were reviewed and property was sold, as in the instance of the town malt mill. A bigger and better town hall must have been planned but the French Revolution and Napoleonic Wars intervened. Finally a committee was appointed and an announcement placed in the Macclesfield Courier 1st. December 1821:

'The house and premises formerly in the possession of the late Mr. Cockson in Mill Street in this Town have been purchased by John Ryle, (Junior) Esq. for the Corporation. The ground plot comprises nearly a statute acre of land, and we understand it is in contemplation to erect a new and elegant Town Hall upon the front site of the present buildings and a New Gaol at the back.

It is hoped that the County will make a liberal allowance towards the erection of the Gaol: the immense and increasing population of this district renders it absolutely necessary that the County Magistrates should have a place of safety for prisoners whilst under examination, at present prosecutors are put to great inconvenience and expense and the ends of Justice are not unfrequently defeated for worst of it'.

The original gaol is said to have been in Dog Lane (now the Mall from the Market Place to the Indoor Market). It appears to have been relocated behind where the Chicken Spit premises now stand, probably at the time of the reassembly of the Foxwist Hall in the Market Place in 1358. From this time onward it was known as the 'King's Gaol' and stood for centuries on a strip of land belonging to the Lord of the Manor of Macclesfield and not the Borough. It was leased out and the jailer was entitled to the profits from the 'business'. There was a dispute in the mid-18th century when a retiring mayor tried to take over the building with the intention of turning it into a button manufactory!

The plot and property purchased on behalf of the Corporation by John Ryle for the new town hall site, had been purchased at an auction held in the Macclesfield Arms on 26th November 1821. It comprised a house, stable, yard, outbuildings and plot of land which extended down Backwallgate. It was close by the gaol and to the north of the castle site on Mill St. and had been occupied by Thomas Cockson, a surgeon who had died, hence the sale.

One wonders what sort of character Cockson was. He owned also (Deed of 1809) premises on the old castle site, part of which he leased out, but evidently retained a summer house, stable and land for his own use. A good deal of controversy had arisen with his neighbours, in particular with the Robinsons who owned houses on Backwallgate and operated a coal carrier's business. When Joshua Robinson prepared his will on 27th July, 1798 he specifically included 'and it is likewise my mind and will that the above premises (the houses on Backwallgate) should not either be sold or let or by any means disposed of to Dr. Cockson of Macclesfield.'

On 11th October 1822 the Town Hall Committee made a contract with Samuel Lake of Alfred Place, Bedford Square, London to build the new public premises for £4,579 under the direction of Francis Goodwin, Esq. 'appointed Architect to the Corporation'.

In the meantime events had moved on apace and the premises purchased by John Ryle on Mill St. were not to be utilised. Also it had been decided to sell the old gaol. The Corporation Minutes for Friday, 29th March 1822 record 'That the Mayor be authorized to sell the Gaol House premises on best Terms and at such time as he shall think proper – with all its imperfections as to title'. This is interesting because the heir to the land on which it stood should have been Lord Cholmondeley, but in 1788 he had decided to auction off all the land relating to the Manor of Macclesfield, as it was heavily mortgaged. In the event the only exception was the Savage Chapel adjoining St. Michael's Church,

The splendid Town Hall built 1823-24 looking at its original entrance, facing St. Michael's churchyard. How different the town centre would have been today if the construction of this building had taken place as originally intended. Perhaps Castle Street would have been constructed a little further to the south in order to open up the vista to the Corinthian columns.

so this little strip of land accommodating the gaol evidently had a very complex question of ownership relating to it. Fortunately for the Corporation it seems possible that young Lord Cholmondeley overlooked the premises assuming the gaol belonged to the Borough, as he had only recently inherited the parkland etc. from his uncle, General Cholmondley.

At the same Corporation meeting it was also recorded 'That the Contract made for the purchase of the late Mr. Cockson's premises be transferred to Mr. James Sargent, he paying the expenses already incurred by the Corporation.' Had the original site be used for the construction of the new town hall how very different would be the appearance of the present town centre today.

The old guildhall (replaced by a splendid town hall with Ionic columns in 1823-24) had been in the joint ownership of the Earl of Derby, on behalf of the Crown, and Macclesfield Corporation.

When the ancient hall of the Black Prince had been replaced in the Tudor Period by this guildhall the Corporation felt strongly that the Mayor's Court was deliberately being eclipsed by the Crown Courts under the control of the Earl of Derby as Steward of the Crown. Amazingly a dispute arose regarding the arrangements for access to the guildhall key, with various officials attempting to lock each other out!

Finally under Elizabeth I a legal ruling was obtained whereby the Mayor and Burgesses appear to have been allowed the right to hold court without the presence of the steward (as previously) and to have their own key. It was specified, however, that the Mayor's court could only have jurisdiction over purely borough matters and their own burgesses, so that is any 'foreigners' were involved then the matter had to be referred to the Crown court.

More power must have been gained by the Mayor's Court during the Parliamentarian Pe-

The town hall extension completed in November 1992. Circumstantial evidence suggests that this was the site of a green, until the late 17th century, with some buildings on three sides but open to Jordangate. From that time onwards the area rapidly developed, with the Jordangate portion becoming especially congested with residents in the mid-18th century, to cope with the influx of workers attracted by Charles Roe's silk enterprise.

The area in which the leisure complex and bowling green were sited by the Corporation in the late 17th century.

riod, for the 7th Earl of Derby was executed in 1651 and his lands sequestrated. It is evident that after the Restoration in 1660 procedures had changed. By 1740, John Stafford, who was firstly Deputy Steward and then Steward of the Hallmote Court, held sessions on behalf of the Crown in his home, Cumberland House on Jordangate. On occasion the Manor and Forest Court was held in the house of John Davenport, Esq., known as the Red Lion in Macclesfield Forest.

So it appears that the Mayor, Aldermen and Burgesses of Macclesfield had succeeded in establishing their authority in their own territory i.e. the borough, and also in claiming precedent for the use of the guildhall, hence their alterations to the building in the late 17th century.

The market place was already the central focus for the town and the guildhall occupied a prime position at the N.E. corner, albeit on a very small site, which surprisingly marked the start of Jordangate.

The only suitable site becoming available for the intended new town hall was a plot on Mill St. purchased in November 1821, but few seemed happy with the choice. During the previous two years the Corporation had purchased several old properties around the Market Place with the intention of demolishing them in order to open up and extend the area, thus continuing the work of a generation earlier.

It so happened that the Mayor for the year 1821-22 was John Wood Hazlehurst, owner of several properties in close proximity to the guildhall. Just how public spirited his delayed offer of these properties to the Corporation was, is difficult to judge. The site on Mill St. had cost £1,670. Mr. Hazlehurst agreed a sum of £2,300 for his holdings. He was paid £200 with the remaining £2,100 negotiated as a loan plus interest payable to him (this would repesent a value of approximately a quarter of a million pounds today).

Amongst the buildings demolished to make way for the Georgian town hall was the Old King's Bakehouse. The original one noted in the Domesday Survey must have been close by the water corn mill but was possibly moved into the centre of town about the same time as the Black Prince's hall was erected in the Market Place in the mid-14th century. It was built near but not next to the hall for fear of fire.

By the late 17th century, when the Tudor guild hall was modernised, the presence of a fire engine stationed at the rear of the building appears to have encouraged development of the area which, within a few years became very congested.

In the 1690s the Corporation provided, what was in effect, a leisure complex on Cuckstoolpit Hill (today the site is just to the east of the River Bollin and Macclesfield railway station). The main feature was a bowling green. Bowls and Macclesfield are almost synonymous, and considering the popularity of the game in Elizabethan England, it must already have been established in the town.

Taking into consideration the layout of buildings etc. the original green was more-than-likely in the area now occupied by the town hall extension completed in November 1992. There Morris dancers would have performed and May Day celebrations taken place and games played.

The Tudor guildhall was obviously demolished, along with other buildings, to make way for the new town hall, so that by 18th August 1823 the Corporation assembled in the Town Clerk's office (presumably in his own home). The foundation-stone was laid on 4th September 1823 and by October, Corporation meetings were taking place in the National School on Duke St. with occasional ones held in the more congenial surroundings of the Macclesfield Arms Hotel on Jordangate!

One would be forgiven for thinking, 'What – no controversy?' but by February 1828 Mr. Hilton, late Clerk of Works for the project, had brought an action against the Corporation Committee who had signed the contract with the London builder, Samuel Lake, 'for arrears of salary and incidental charges'. The Corporation submitted an appeal, intended a defence and asked for full details of the claim as soon as possible; the

outcome is not known.

With the completion of the town hall the first police station was incorporated in its cellars. An artist's drawing of 1850 clearly shows railings running along the Churchside of the building over which people could look down into an elongated well which accommodated the stairs leading down to the impressive police station entrance.

By 1869 further enlargement was necessary which was fortunately executed in a style conforming to the original classical style of architecture. This extension created the present projecting portico supported by further Ionic columns, presenting a new facade towards Chestergate. The old council chamber was utilised for committee rooms and a new one created together with the Mayor's parlour and Magistrates' room.

Further reconstruction and refurbishment took place including the creation of a dome on iron columns, bringing the total costs to £15,200 which, of course, did not escape criticism.

Since reorganisation in 1974 further extensions have been necessary to accommodate a greater number of personnel under one roof. The Borough of Macclesfield now covers 200 square miles and roughly coincides with the old Hundred and Manor and Forest. When the burgesses of Macclesfield started their bid for independence in the 13th century they could never have imagined that some day their powers would extend to cover all those Crown lands, nor could they have visualised the considerable number of employees required to maintain those powers.

The Holly and The Ivy

With the approach of the Festive Season I am once again reminded of how the Christmas Carol 'The Holly and the Ivy' is so appropriate in encapsulating the historical spirit of Macclesfield.

The chorus is a reminder of the winter sun rising over the Hollins and Shutlingsloe, with the deer running through Macclesfield Forest and the Chase (one of the favourite hunting grounds of the Royal Family, particularly in the 13th and early 14th centuries). The 'merry organ' and choir conveniently relate to St. Michael's Parish Church, formerly a Parochial Chapel founded by Queen Eleanor of Castile which, in varying forms, has dominated its 'friendly' crag for more than 700 years, and produced the early musical inspiration for the area. It is easy to imagine the 'sweet singing' of the original choir of young school boys in the early 16th century, particularly at Evensong, under the leadership of their Catholic priest and schoolmaster.

The verses of the carol, of course, specifically refer to the holly tree and the ivy. The tree (Ilex Aquifolium) is the most important English evergreen and many excellent specimens can be found in Macclesfield's parks and surrounding countryside. It is especially associated with Christmas when it is seen at its best enhanced with red berries. For centuries holly has been used to decorate holy places, yet the origin of this custom remains obscure.

The Romans are known to have sent holly boughs to friends with other gifts during the festival of Saturnalia, which began mid-December; whilst the Druids used all forms of evergreens to decorate their dwellings during winter periods. The congregations of Christian churches continued the idea of using holly boughs predominantly as decoration; some old Church calendars were noted 'Templa Exorantur' against Christmas Eve, which is translated as 'Churches are decked'. Another school of thought suggests that the prickly leaves and red berries symbolize the crown of thorns and drops of blood of Christ, hence in some northen European countries the tree is named 'Christ's thorn'.

The holly is a slow growing tree yet grows larger in Britain than anywhere else in Europe, especially where the soil is rich and sandy as in the Macclesfield area.

The wood is white, hard and compact, much favoured by wood turners and was possibly the encouragement for a Quaker, with the delightful name of Micajah Wortley (or Worsley), to set up his shop near Parsonage Green (today Park Green): a deed of 1735 refers to him as a 'Chairemaker' which would also include making stools and small items.

His lease was one of several Quaker leases on the land known as 'Pickford Eyes' which ran from Waters Green to Parsonage Green and from the River Bollin to part way along Mill St. The reason for this appears to be because 'Jedidiah' Pickford, a Quaker merchant of Bristol, who brought tobacco from Virginia and Maryland, was trustee of the land on behalf of his young nephew, from 1689 to 1697. Micajah also leased 'Hallowes Meadow' which seems to have been close by the Hollyfields (deed 1704) or Halleyfields (today near Brook St.)

Holly tree wood is mentioned occasionally in 17th inventories for the area and would be an ideal material from which to make silk button moulds; these were then covered with scraps of fabric and embroidered with threads of silk, mohair and ox hair.

Surprisingly the ivy is also a tree, though we are used to its forms of bush and creeper. It has been associated with the holly in decorating churches for centuries. Its favourite habitat is

The holly tree in the centre of the photo, growing beside the pathway of St. Paul's churchyard, is one of many magnificent specimens which can be seen in and around the Macclesfield area, encouraged by the rich and sandy soil.

The present Ivy House on Park Lane, the site of some earlier buildings which were described as old in the late 18th century. Note the interesting patterns in the brickwork of No. 112 and 114 Park Lane which date from 1795 and would have continued along the facade of the original Ivy House.

loss or damage by fire, periodic painting of the external woodwork and the paving of the new street to 5ft in depth and 4 inches high. Clulow's surveyor was to carry out periodic inspections, whilst Orme was to keep the necessary soughs and drains in good repair with appropriate scouring and cleansing.

Four long and narrow buildings seem to have been built, which would eventually take up the numbers 112 to 118 Park Lane, although the latter was only just over 10ft wide and possibly had an entrance on Hobson St. This property was retained by the Orme family, passing down to David Orme by 1878 when it is clearly shown on a plan dated 24th July as 'IVY HOUSE'. More than likely it had been used as a small cotton warehouse or manufactory before its conversion into a very small public house and dwelling (O.S. Map 1871).

Nos. 112 and 114 were one unit owned by John Pimblott and still retain a very interesting pattern in their brickwork, just below the gutterings; the frontage was 27ft 4 inches which today is divided between the two properties; 112 being just over 12ft and 114 almost 15ft The remaining property 116 belonged to William Day with a frontage of again almost 15ft

In order to accommodate the present public house on site, still known as the Ivy House, No. 116 and the old Ivy House were combined, but this only gives a frontage of exactly 27ft yet the present frontage is 33ft The obvious explanation is that the 5ft wide pavement, running along the side of the old Ivy House on Hobson St. was built over and a new pavement laid, which today has added to the very restrictive access to and from Park Lane.

One can only assume that the original Ivy House was covered with ivy, yet even without, the present facade adds to the character of Park Lane but 'Of all the trees that are in the wood, The holly bears the crown' – MERRY CHRISTMAS

old ruined buildings where it can climb happily over stones and masonry, reaching great heights by tenaciously winding around drainpipes etc. and spreading across brick walls. It is a plant which is again becoming popular, despite its contraversial 'press' on occasion, when arguments rage as to whether it creates damp in walls or actually helps to keep them dry.

Built on land which once belonged to the parkland of Macclesfield, the Ivy House on Park Lane is an obvious choice for the role relative to the carol. Before 1793 the plot was much larger, being just over 52ft wide along Park Lane and 76ft in length along what is now Hobson St.

Henry Orme, a cotton spinner, leased the land and buildings from John Clulow, which included an old (farm) house, barn and cow 'house'. Orme was given permission to pull down all the old buildings and build 'one or more good & substantial' houses or other building of 'good well burnt brick' etc. but on the site of the previous buildings; the work had to be completed by 29th September 1795 and to cost not less than £200! The intended new street, unnamed but now Hobson St. was also noted in the deeds.

The planning stipulations were very impressive including the necessity for insurance from

New Year – balloon trips and Roe's Liverpool smelter

Two hundred and thirty years ago an important industrialist by the name of Charles Roe of Macclesfield had at last gained a foothold on Liverpool soil.

The smelthouses in Toxteth Park, Liverpool depicted at the foot of Charles Roe's monument in Christ Church, Macclefield. The original Liverpool smelter began operations on New Year's Day 1768 but on the South Shore. (Photo courtesy of the Churches Conservation Trust).

The bitter disappointment of a failed scheme to bring a canal through Macclesfield as part of a greater plan linking the Mersey Estuary to the Midlands and elsewhere, had made him more determined than ever to seek an alternative solution for his business interests.

The intrigues and plotting by the Duke of Bridgewater, who seduced Josiah Wedgwood and his Dissenting associates into supporting his scheme, is beyond the scope of this article. However, it is sufficient to say that one of the key reasons for the unmarried Duke's apparent vindictiveness appears to stem from the fact that he had been jilted three times, and one of his former fiancées had married George Warren of Poynton. As Warren was an enthusiastic and powerful supporter of the Macclesfield Scheme, considering it essential for transporting coal from his collieries, the Duke was hardly likely to assist his former adversary in gaining financial rewards and also anyone who happened to be associated with him.

By 1767 the Macclesfield Copper Company established by Charles Roe was buying ore in large quantities from Cornwall supplemented by North Wales, and all conveyed via the Port of Liverpool. A canal would have greatly facilitated the carriage of these ores to Macclesfield but as this had been denied, Charles Roe decided on an alternative. The most logical course was to smelt the copper in Liverpool, which greatly reduced the bulk, and to send it up the Weaver as bars or pigs for refining on Macclesfield Common.

Liverpool Corporation had become a very powerful body with a stranglehold on large areas of land particularly along the sea shore and 'foreigners' stood no chance of obtaining leases, so the alternative was to work through one of the freemen of the town. Charles Roe's successful partnership with a member of Liverpool Corporation saw the company busily building a fine modern copper works on the Liverpool South Shore during the summer months of 1767. On New Year's Day 1768 production began and one can well imagine the satisfaction felt by everyone connected with the enterprise. Charles Roe's eldest son, William, at only 21 years of age was sent from Macclesfield to take overall charge, not only of the works but of all the supplies arriving at the port for the company.

Unfortunately another upheaval was about to take place due to the death of Charles Roe's Liverpool partner. Behind the scenes the enemy attacked once more, using the Liverpool press with its Dissenting establishment and friends of the Wedgwood fraternity. The result was a move for the smeltworks along the Mersey Estuary and into Toxteth Park, where for the next 20 years William Roe would successfully manage operations.

Although William's roots were still in Macclesfield, the town of Liverpool was his second home, and slowly but surely the Macclesfield influence began to take effect. It is interesting to note the comment of one historian who deduced that the majority of burgesses in Liverpool were Whig until 1780 and then 'surprisingly the town became more Tory', but he had reckoned without the Macclesfield contingent!

On rare occasions news items from Macclesfield featured in the Liverpool press and one can imagine that stories from the port were recounted in Macclesfield as the Roe family and their employees journeyed to and fro.

Just as today, balloon fever was on the increase and the famous Mr. Lunardi appeared in Liverpool during the summer of 1785 to attempt a remarkable balloon flight. There is little doubt that William and wife Hannah, together with their five surviving young children all under the age of nine years (two had died), and baby Frances of four months would have joined the crowds who flocked to see the extraordinary feat. Although the attempt took place in mid-summer the story is well worth the telling.

The flight was to begin at the New Fort in Liverpool with a balloon made from oiled silk on Wednesday 20th July, but when Mr. Lunardi went to the building where his precious transporter was suspended, to his 'unspeakable Mortification' he found that it had fallen to the ground 'with the Top entirely blown out owing to the Man who fills it with Atmospheic Air forcing too great a Quantity into it'. Several people were set to work to repair it and by the following day he had received more oiled silk from the town and the balloon was made as 'Staunch as ever'.

On Friday 22nd July at 2 o'clock Lunardi ordered a gun to be fired as a signal that the balloon was once again being filled. Another gun was fired at 5 o'clock when he judged that sufficient air had been pumped in, at which time he attached a little 'Gallery' only 4ft square but bedecked lightly with blue silk valances and a gold fringe. At precisely 6 o'clock he climbed into the basket, donned his 'Regimentals' and five minutes later signalled the firing of the third gun then rose slowly upwards into the air.

Lunardi was delighted with the scene below and likened the masts of the ships, which were covered with human beings, to mulberry trees

in Italy at the time when the silkworms 'begin to construct their little temporary Sepulchres'. Crowds covered the west side of the Ladies' Walk and all the important buildings, whilst those on the shore completely hid the yellow sands from view. After eulogising on the magnificence of Liverpool and its commerce he drifted gently onwards until 28 minutes past 6, when he enjoyed the most beautiful view of the town. Having decided to ascend, Lunardi took off and threw away his military jacket and 'rofe majeftically' towards the southwest.

He viewed the Irish Sea covered in cloud but with the bright sun shining above and then turned north and at 45 minutes past 6 saw a thunder cloud. The thermometer was recording 32 degrees, so as a last resource Lunardi's waistcoat followed his jacket. Five minutes later and about two miles up, with the thermometer at 27, unsurprisingly Lunardi found himself suffering greatly from the cold. The snow from the top of the balloon had melted with the heat from the hot air, but on running down to the neck had frozen, this Lunardi shook off causing the balloon to rise but the temperature to fall by only 1 degree.

Within a minute Lunardi began to descend and the temperature rose quite quickly; now he was about ³/₄ mile above ground when his speed increased sharply and he saw several people on horseback following, but on a wrong road. 'I then drew back my Grapple, for fear of catching hold of fome Trees, and finally defsended at fix Minutes past Seven, in a Corn Field near Symmonds-Wood, about Twelve Miles from Liverpool'.

Chester racecourse in the summer of 1996, the balloon was about to make its maiden voyage with the author on board! It brought back happy memories of Lunardi, but he did not have to contend with air traffic from Liverpool and Manchester airports and could make his attempt to the north of the Mersey Estuary.

Pickford Family

We are all guilty, to a greater or lesser degree, of regarding history as a subject which relates to things that we really have very little connection with. We often talk about the past as though it was taking place on another planet, but the people involved were our ancestors and it is through them that our lives are as they are today. It is vital that we do not lose sight of the past links in the chain, so that in forging those of the present and future we avoid creating weak ones; besides which it makes life far more interesting.

Looking towards Wildboarclough and the Black Combes where the Pickford family kept a considerable number of sheep and several hogs. They were tanners and malsters by trade but also became involved in the wool trade and later made a fortune in the Lancashire cotton trade.

Research can reveal some fascinating relationships which at first appear totally unconnected. For instance, how is the sponsorship of a particular weather forecast on television by a large holiday company, related to Pickford St. in Macclesfield? Through the intricate threads of history we shall find out.

The story begins (so the Pickford family were pleased to relate) in a remote medieval hamlet called King Sterndale in Derbyshire, not far from Buckstones (today Buxton) where the family had settled for several generations. From there they gradually spread into Edale, the Stockport area and certainly during the reign of Elizabeth I a Thomas Pickford was attending Prestbury Parish Church. In 1612 the baptism of another Thomas, the apparent grandson of the first, heralded a strong connection with the township of Macclesfield; although young Thomas is eventually recorded as living in Mottram (St.) Andrew, on a property deed of 7th February, 1655 he is also shown to be an Alderman of Macclesfield. This date, of course, coincides with the middle of the Parliamentarian period.

To become an alderman or burgess of Macclesfield one had to be in possession of part or a whole burgage plot within the Borough and later evidence suggests that the Pickford burgage was on the site now occupied by the NatWest. Bank on the corner of Chestergate and the Market Place (scene of a much later incident when, in 1745, one of Bonnie Prince Charlie's men was stabbed through the thigh in the shop then occupying the corner site. See page 41).

Thomas, together with James Pickford the younger, in 1655 leased a share of the 'annual rents, tolls (excepting Fair-tolls), stallage, booths' and premises in Macclesfield from the Mayor and Aldermen.

James's father, James the elder is first recorded in Macclesfield during the reign of James I and was Mayor of the Borough 1626/27 (2nd. year of Charles I's reign) The circumstantial evidence suggests a very close relationship

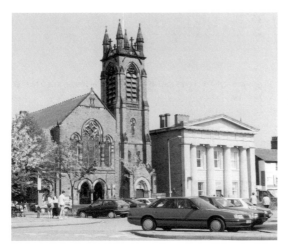

Park Green looking towards the western boundary of the waste land purchased by James Pickford the younger from the Mayor of Macclesfield in 1655. On that boundary stood Pickford Hall and the most likely site (by a process of elimination) was where the United Reform Church stands today. The hall was later pulled down by Charles Roe when he expanded his silk premises.

between Thomas and James the elder. On 8th November 1641 James the elder had leased a cottage, tenements and land in Back Street from three burgesses and on 20th April 1642 another burgage from Earl Rivers for four shillings a year on Jordangate Street. This latter rental must relate to premises on the site occupied by the Bull's Head Hotel today. In 1646 James the elder gifted the property to his son, James the younger, to establish a fortune and security for the family.

The family were tanners and malsters and great opportunists, soon to diversify into wool and cotton. James the elder had been involved in a dispute during 1629 when he had set up a handmill or quern in Wildboarclough and supplied malt from Derby to the inhabitants of the Borough (see article June 1996) and thereby made a considerable profit. It is this Pickford who encouraged the growth of brewhouses in Macclesfield and it is interesting to note that some of the Pickford holdings (which would shortly include the Old Castle site on Mill Street) were, in due course, sites of the Castle Inn, the Bull's Head, the Angel Inn and the Royal Oak, the latter on Back Street (now King Edward Street – since writing this article the name has changed to Maxwells).

Thomas's branch of the family appear to have become involved in the Poynton and Stockport areas at this time, leaving James the younger and his son, Jonathan to acquire as much property as possible in the Borough and also in the Manor and Forest of Macclesfield.

One of the most important purchases by James the younger was a piece of 'waste' land from the Mayor of Macclesfield on 10th July 1655; it comprised the Lower and Higher Eyes, soon to be known as Pickford Eyes, which originally had been two ancient enclosures of the medieval period. The area today roughly covers the land on both sides of Sunderland Street from the River Bollin to Mill Street. The N.E. boundary followed the upper part of Pickford Street, then turning to continue through the supermarket building of Giant and along a line to include the bus station site and also the block containing the Queen's Hotel premises. It then cut across Waters Green to the River Bollin. The S.W. area was bounded by Park Green (then known as Parsonage Green) and somewhere on the northern side of the Green stood Pickford Hall. Unfortunately the deeds for the United Reform Church site are at present unavailable, but from other evidence this would appear to be the site on which the hall stood. (see subsequent page 113).

Jonathan Pickford moved to Ashton-under-Lyne where the family became involved in cotton mills etc. especially in Royton, but when he died in 1690 his holdings in Macclesfield included the house containing a bedstead and bedding, a chest, four chairs and table, a stool, fire irons a shovel and tongs, two more tables and most importantly a coffer and wool, the latter two items with a substantial value of £24 3s. which today would be at least £3,000. In the forest at 'The Nabs' was the handmill, two old bedsteads, two beds and an old table and gun, 165 old sheep, 3 lambs, 20 hogs, one bull and a bullock. His grandfather, James, had leased 300 acres of land a building and farmhouse but how this compares with Jonathan's holdings is difficult to say. Jonathan's lands are recorded as 67 acres at Harrop, 22 acres at Black Combes from the Earl of Derby, various leases from Earl Rivers which included the Dams and lands in Sutton, thus consolidating an area around the western side of Pickford Eyes and a lease of a half moss room in Macclesfield Park. There was a house and buildings on Mill Street with 2 crofts at the rear (the Castle site) and a house on Back Street leased directly from Edward Swettenham to his father James. The latter was more-than-likely a renewal of the earlier lease of 1641 which would have been a sublease from Swettenham's tenants.

An interesting note in the will stipulates that each week, in order to 'satisfy' his grandfather's will, 52 shillings had to be distributed to the Poor of Macclesfield at or near the corner of Chestergate, which presumably meant outside the Pickford burgage.

With all their business contacts there was one thing which the Pickfords had learnt, how to transport goods to various parts.

Before continuing the Pickford story I must mention that I have been unable trace the date of death of James the elder. There was a note amongst deeds which simply reads '20th Dec. 1646 James the elder to his son James the younger all his goods and chattels in his Macclesfield house'. Unable to trace the probate or date of death I originally took this to be the date on which the will was proved. However, I overlooked the fact that subsequently I discovered James the elder as mayor of Macclesfield yet again in 1652/53. Therefore the 1646 date must relate to either preparation of the will or a gift (?) of property. He does not appear to have lived much longer than the year of his mayoralty, but as many historians know the Interregnum Period (1649-1660) is notorious for its dearth of records.

It is sufficient to briefly mention that the main line of the Pickfords continued through Jonathan of Ashton-under-Lyne whose grandson Joseph (born 1709) entered into a marriage of great significance with Mary Radcliffe in 1740. Macclesfield property was part of the marriage settlement and, whether by accident or design, that which was only leased, not owned, was also included; this was later withdrawn and replaced by Lancashire properties.

The Radcliffe family of Milnesbridge House in Yorkshire could boast of high ranking army officers amongst their male progeny.

Joseph and Mary's son Joseph became a promoter of the Rochdale Canal in the early 1790s. This son's second marriage to Miss Elizabeth Sunderland of Croydon (from yet another Yorkshire family) gave rise to the name Sunderland Street in Macclesfield.

Joseph inherited the estate of his uncle William Radcliffe, but only by assuming the surname and arms of Radciffe by Royal permission on 19th December 1795. He was created Baronet, 2nd November 1813 for 'his prompt

Premises on King Edward St. (formerly Back St.) until recently a public house known as 'The Royal Oak'. In 1788 there was a coachhouse and barn behind the dwellinghouse which, together with adjoining premises were used by Pickford & Co. waggoners as part of their nationwide network. As Manchester mail was rerouted through Macclesfield from March 1787 and Matthew Pickford provided horses and riders, this appear to be the site of the first official central Post Office in the town.

and judicious exertions as a magistrate during a period of insubordination, danger and alarm, in the year 1812' (brought about by food shortages etc. due to Napoleon's scheme of blockading continental ports).

The family were ardent members of St. Michael's Parish Church in Ashton-under-Lyne, a church said to have some of the finest medieval glass windows of any parish church in the country. There they owned several pews and the future Baronet's son, at that time still a Pickford but yet another Joseph, was Ordained Deacon in 1790. This young man's unfortunate death at 37 years of age left his only son and heir, Joseph (!) aged almost 5 years, to succeed to the Baronetcy on the death of his grandfather in 1819, when he was nearly 20 years of age.

There is now another twist to the Pickford story; whereas Quakerism almost overtook part of the family in the late 17th century, with the marriage of Sir Joseph, 2nd. Bart. to Jacobina

Maria, youngest daughter of Capt. John Macdonnell, it would appear that part of the family were converted to Roman Catholicism.

Amongst their numerous descendants are high ranking army officers, a 'Gentleman-in-Waiting to H.H. The Pope' and of recent date a Dominican friar. (I am grateful to Father Abbott, Historian of the Shrewsbury Diocese for drawing my attention to this latter information).

We now return to a James Pickford who married Martha Johnson at Capesthorne Hall Chapel on 18th August 1740. Could he be the James born 1710, grandson of Jonathan, Ashton-under-Lyne, who for some inexplicable reason on 10th September 1729 allowed his nephew Joseph (who married Mary Radcliffe) to take over many property leases in Macclesfield? Unfortunately doubt sets in because of the predominating Christian names Thomas and Matthew (apart from James of course) in this branch of the family. Yet circumstantial evidence does support a relationship which is frustratingly elusive at present.

James became a Manchester to London waggoner, known to be operating by August 1756, apparently having moved from Adlington to Poynton in 1747 when he leased a large farm from Sir George Warren. There waggons could be repaired and the valuable horses catered for. The growth of the business is well documented elsewhere and was eventually inherited by son Matthew, who succeeded his mother in 1772 aged 32 years. Matthew's 27 years at the helm saw a substantial expansion by road and canal; when he died in 1799 he was considered to be 'one of the most extensive proprietors of the carrying business in the country'. (In 1775 he had joined a group of innkeepers to run a coach service to London which had expanded to other major cities by 1785. It is interesting to note that the pick-up point for passengers in Manchester was the Upper Royal Oak.)

It is this Matthew whose name appears on the deeds of, what was until quite recently, the Royal Oak on King Edward St. The date 6th June 1788 indicates that Matthew Snr. was already in occupation of the premises which comprised a dwellinghouse, coachhouse and barn, (further details see page 106-108) by which date his services to London had risen from 2 to 3 each week in 1777 (taking 4 and a half days), to a daily service Monday to Saturday. By 1817 the network is estimated to have involved 1,000 horses, and the time for the 186 miles between London and Manchester cut to one third.

As Macclesfield received the postal concession for Manchester in March 1787 it suggests that, in effect, the Royal Oak site was the first official central Post Office in Macclesfield, as Matthew Pickford provided horses and riders for the daily postal service. The brightly coloured coach was specially designed to travel at great speed, complete with post horn and armed guard. As the coach rapidly approached each turnpike the horn was blown as a signal for the gates to be flung wide open so as not to impede the passage of the mail.

This was an extremely lucrative business and therefore a concession jealously fought over. Matthew did not retain it too long, but the money provided capital for his further expansion into canal conveyancing.

Canal barges moored alongside The Red Bull public house Buglawton. Before the completion of the Macclesfield Canal, in the early 19th century, Pickford & Co. used the nearby wharf as a terminal for goods sent by canal to and from the Midlands and London.

Archaeological dig
Manchester Airport

An exciting opportunity arose this month (April 1998) which simply could not be missed.

Manchester Airport: scene of the archaeological dig taking place on the site of the proposed second runway. Until recent date this area was under the jurisdiction of the Hundred of Macclesfield; if taking into account its shortlived precursor, the Hundred of Hamestan, and its successor, Macclesfield Borough Council, it is an association which had lasted for almost a thousand years.
Note in the foreground a reconstruction of a Bronze Age wickerwork fence.

I received a media invitation to visit part of the site of Manchester Airport's proposed second runway, where an archaeological dig was taking place, and joined a small group of journalists who were trying to establish when the Mesolithic Period existed.

Mesolithic – 10,000 B.C. to 4,000 B.C., but easier to understand when items are said to be at least 6,000 years old. Very impressive!

A short bus ride took us to the site which covers just over one hectare (i.e. 2.75 acres) and runs alongside the still extant Altrincham Rd. It is in the proximity of where the 'Old Brick Yard' (Jackson's) used to be; a favourite viewing area for plane spotters, now moved to an even better position.

When work began last year the area at first appeared to contain little of archaeological interest, even after a geophysics survey along what had turned out to be a gravel ridge, always of interest from an agricultural point of view.

The huge task of straightening part of the River Bollin's tortuous meanderings, not far distant from the area, revealed a wooden trackway together with a shoe and clog; the latter are undergoing preservation and dating, whilst analysis of the logs from the former gives a date of 1737 for the tree felling.

Returning to the main site, subsequent demolition of the 18th century Oversley Farm-house brought to light footings of a 17th century building so, keen to find any waste pits (middens) which can hold an absolute wealth of information for the trained observor, a trial trench was dug across the adjoining gravel ridge. Intuition paid off and the first indications of a Bronze Age farmstead began to emerge, date – somewhere between 2,000 B.C. to 700 B.C. Contingencies for just such a find, despite an initial lack of evidence, had been incorporated into the plans, so it was 'full-steam ahead' for the team of 15 archaeologists from one of

Prehistoric finds on display at the Oversley Farm site mostly relating to the Bronze Age period 2,000 B.C. to 700 B.C. The complete beaker is a reproduction based on some of the shards found during excavations. There is a batch of worked flints from an even earlier period, the Mesolithic, which dates them as at least 6,000 years old.

only two construction companies in the country large enough to provide such a service.

Trenching now took place at intervals across the whole area during the summer and autumn of 1997 with some interesting results, and still continues apace until Easter. Only one 'clearly defined area' has produced an abundance of the earliest (Mesolithic) worked flints but, as expected, no evidence of any structures remain; mesolithic man was a normadic hunter never staying too long in one place.

Mesolithic sites tend to be stream or riverside locations and close by meres or lakes, features with which Cheshire has been well endowed during its unique history. In the early 1990s only three flints in the ploughsoil of Tatton Park were the precursor to a Mesolithic site which eventually produced around 900 flints, confirming much hunting activity in the area.

Remains from individuals know an Lindow Man I, II & III (it is suspected that I and III are the same male) are much later, attributed to the Iron Age which followed the Bronze and more specifically, with the help of radiocarbon dating for the fragments of III only, about 200 B.C. These relate to Lindow Common, formerly known as Lindow Moss, but situated to the south of Bollin Valley not to the north as Oversley Farm. A 19th century discovery of a trackway and skeleton of a boar on the Common were only briefly recorded at the time without details of location, so typical of late Victorian historiology.

Fortunately with present day dedication the infinite details relating to the Oversley Farm site have been meticulously recorded and suggest the following: the whole Bronze Age settlement was enclosed by a ditch with a wickerwork fence rising from its inner lip, but allowing a sufficient gap at the southern end to indicate an entrance (i.e. at the opposite end from where Oversley Farm was eventually built). A further ditch dissects the site from north to south suggesting an enclosure for domestic animals.

The eastern portion contains some residual evidence to imply the presence of Bronze Age hearths and two round houses which would have had thatched roofs. Two important items are small pieces of possible copper slag, yet to be analysed in the hope of proving a connection with the Alderley Mines.

The western portion appears to have contained a long house, granary and further hearth. The midden was outside the enclosure but adjoining the ditch to the west of the entrance and abutting Altrincham Rd. which suggests that a prehistoric track might have originally followed the line of the road.

The midden and hearths yielded charred barley, hazelnuts and part of a probable quernstone. Elsewhere a knife blade and arrow head have been discovered by chance in other parts of the runway site.

The dearth of appropriate artefacts on site leaves an intriguing gap after the demise of the Bronze Age farm. Only a couple of Romano-British pottery shards, a brooch from the 2nd. century A.D. and a few possible Iron Age artefacts (dating yet to be determined) link the centuries from the Bronze to the 17th, apart from a very small scattering of mediaeval fragments over a large area of ploughed soil, but not sufficient in number to prove actual occupation of the site. This is a usual pattern because farming activities in more modern times have tended to destroy tangible evidence of the Roman and mediaeval periods.

From ground level the first impression of the Manchester Airport Runway 2 archaeological dig site, with the whole of its topsoil removed, was one of blankness and vast desolation. How could anyone relate to the past in such a place?

Before first stepping into the area a visit was made to the tent-like structure erected over the site of the Oversley Farm-house, to view several of the artefacts recovered from the dig. First to meet the eye were the remains of a magnificent 17th century slipware dish (plate) some 32cm. (12ins) in diameter, covered with a bright orange lead glaze and decorated with a pale yellow ochre slip. This find alone was enough to bring the whole area to life and put the dig in perspective.

Alongside a 17th century silver buckle, James II coin and substantial portions of two superbly potted vessels (all recovered from waste pits) there was a table neatly displaying some of the prehistoric artefacts already referred to. Instantly the site took on new meaning and from a high observation platform at the far end nearest the A538, aided by an artist's impression of a Bronze Age farmstead and various helpful indicators strategically placed by the team of diggers, it was possible to reconstruct in one's mind (without too much imagination), what the scene would have looked like all those centuries ago.

At present no evidence of Tudor buildings has appeared, allowing me to deduce that the 17th century dwellers probably thought they were building on virgin land. At that period, because of religious intolerances of one form or another, often a family of one particular persuasion would look for a sympathetic landlord, usually a prominent land owner of the same faith, hoping to obtain building permission or a lease of a property on his land. These dwellings were often in remote areas, giving people a chance to quietly carry on with their lives.

It is interesting to note that to the south of the farm, just over the other side of the Bollin Valley, Burdett's map of 1777 sites a Quaker Meeting House and because of the Pickford family connections with Derby, Quakerism came very early to the area.

By the late 17th century England was entering a period of prosperity, which meant that from the 1740s onwards modernisation and refurbishment of properties was underway. Often fascades were altered but internal features retained, as in the instance of Charles Roe House on Chestergate, Macclesfield. Therefore it is not surprising to discover that the 17th century building on the Oversley Farm site was converted by its 18th occupants in the probable hope of 'keeping up with the Jones's'.

Sadly nothing remained of the 17th century features from which to form a picture of the house, yet the pottery shards, buckle and coin (James II) do point to a family of more than adequate means. Farms in the late 17th and 18th centuries were the insurance for subsistence, but time after time I have discovered that the main source of income was from mercantile business activities.

The superb 17th century dish would have been a treasured possession, no doubt displayed on a heavy oak dresser or table and whoever broke it would have been very upset, unless done by a marauder.

It is known that Bonnie Prince Charlie's men spread out across the countryside on their way from Stockport to Macclesfield in early December 1745 and some came by way of Alderley Edge. Within a few days, whilst hurriedly retreating from Derby, the remnants of the Pretender's army scoured the area for food and took

The display of 17th century artefacts from the Oversley Farm site.

revenge for their bitter disappointment. Tenants at Capesthorne Hall had 17 out of 18 horses stolen, as guns and carts were dragged to Preston, and en route even the coal waggons from the Legh of Lyme collieries in South Lancashire were confiscated. However, one can only speculate on how such a valuable piece of pottery came to be broken and what happened to the missing pieces.

Slipwares originated on the Continent, in particular Germany and Holland and were imported into England in the early 17th century, hardly surprising when considering that the lead for the glazes was sent to Hamburg and Antwerp etc. through the port of Chester from mines in North and Mid-Wales. The search for silver, which proved so successful near Aberystwyth, often produced lead ore containing only small traces of the valuable metal,

The remnants of a superb 17th century dish (plate) of about 32cm. (12ins). The bright orange colour has been trailed with a pale yellow ochre slip to form a floral design, typical of Staffordshire (Burslem) pottery of the period.

too insignificant to retrieve. This lead ore, known as 'Potter's Ore', was considered 'fit only for glazing pottery' (1627). (Silver in normal use does not tarnish, it is the metals with which it combines that cause discolouration e.g. copper).

By the 1650s the potters of Burslem in Staffordshire, appreciating that this was the finest lead ore, were paying the considerable sum of £9 per ton. Their pots were unique, for nowhere else in England was there such a variety of local clays with the convenience of coal seams close by.

Black and red wares were produced, many with red clay bodies, but some with off-white as the Oversley example. Plates were made by the method of press-moulding; in exactly the same way as pastry is rolled out, fitted in a pie dish and trimmed round the edge, so the clay was fitted to the mould. Clay behaves more like hardened plastercene than pastry, making it possible to invert the mold and remove the plate whilst at the same time allowing it to fall face down onto a thick coil of clay to prevent the rim collapsing. The plate was allowed to dry out, then placed in a saggar to protect it from flames, and baked in a kiln at red heat.

The next process was to dip by hand in a lead glaze and refire at a higher temperature. The orange colour of the Oversley plate was difficult and expensive to achieve. An early 19th century recipe shows it was done by mixing litharge (red lead), antimony (a brittle metallic substance of light bluish white) and oxides of tin and iron.

Until the 1630s English potters in general, although copying Continental patterns, had produced very little, but by the mid-century the industry was well established with local designs developing. Staffordshire in particular was renowned for its superb pots with their 'unsophisticated' motifs, done by trailing a thick creamy textured clay across the brightly glazed surface, rather like decorating cakes with icing. There are some fine examples in the Hanley Museum and a small display at Little Moreton Hall.

Another important area of potteries (apart from those in the South of England) was Ticknall near Burton-on-Trent, Derbyshire, but I suspect that the Oversley plate is of Staffordshire origin together with the two large vessels, one of which looks like a bread pot.

These are fine examples of the types of pottery used by the residents of the Macclesfield area c. 1650-1750 and, of course, the Pickford family with their farm-houses at Adlington and elsewhere whose story continues overleaf.

Pickford holdings, Mill Street, Chestergate and Park Green

On the 1756/57 Land Tax Return for Macclesfield Francis Beswick appears as owner of a plot of land, size 1½ acres on Back Street. In modern terms this means just over 3 acres (9 Cheshire acres = 19 statute acres) on King Edward Street. Two years later, on part of the site, he built a very fine 'Mansion House' which is still standing with rainwater heads proudly sporting his initials.

Former Rural District Council building on King Edward St. The half on the left of the photograph, with mock portico (doorway with columns) and a venetian window on either side, is the original 'Mansion House' built by Francis Beswick. The right hand half is much later and takes up the space which formerly led to a yard with stables etc. part of which belonged to the Pickford carriers who occupied the former Royal Oak Inn (just visible with hanging basket and chimney on the extreme right).

Eventually Beswick purchased part of a yard together with buildings, stables etc. at the rear of his premises (today in the backside of Cumberland Street) part of which he sold to his next door neighbour Matthew Pickford for his carrier business.

On 6th June 1788 Matthew obtained a loan from Francis Beswick of £270 at interest for which he gave, as security, the whole of his premises on Back St.

Matthew, of course, died in 1799 (see page 101) having just completed an agreement for a large depot at Paddington, the London terminus of the Grand Junction extension canal. His portion of the business passed to his two sons; Thomas, just 21 years old, and Matthew only 14 years, whose shares were held by his brother until his majority in 1805. The other part of the business was held by the brother of Matthew deceased, another Thomas.

Uncle Thomas had a 500 acre farm in Hertfordshire. He was a noted agriculturalist much preferring hogs to horses and kept a herd of 300 pigs. He also had 350 sheep, a brewery and managed, on occasion, to oversee the carrier business in London. This is so reminiscent of the 17th century Pickford family of Macclesfield and Ashton-under-Lyne with their tanning, wool and malt businesses. Also, though early deeds are missing for the Back Street property, it does seem possible that the cottage, tenements and land are the same premises as those used for the carrier business. leased by James Pickford the elder in 1641 (see page 99) and referred to in his grandson's will of 1690 as a house on Back Street leased from Edward Swettenham. It could be coincidence, yet does beg a close relationship between the two families.

It would seem that by the time of his death in 1799, the elder Matthew had already over-reached himself in order to eclipse the opposition, a situation passed on to his sons and brother, Thomas. But Thomas was a survivor, not having put all his 'eggs in one basket' and his two sons, James, who kept the Castle Inn on Wood St. London and Matthew, who inherited a fortune from an uncle, would all benefit from their diverse business interests.

By 1800 another uncle, Jonathan Higginson, a carrier of Knutsford, came into the firm with 3 shares, whilst each of the four sons held $4\frac{1}{2}$ shares, with the remaining 3 held by other close relatives.

London – Cheapside 18th century – As the artist drew this picture, just behind his left shoulder was Wood St. There, within three blocks, was the Castle Inn used as the London headquarters of Pickford & Co. from 1794 to 1918.

However, an arrangement had been made with Kendal bankers, Messrs, Wilson, Crewdson & Co. who held an account with a London banking house, by which the Pickfords could draw upon their credit for Bills of exchange (i.e. in modern terms, cash cheques). As security the Pickfords offered their premises in Macclesfield and other buildings in Manchester, the City of London and in Paddington (London at that time was very much a collection of villages with the City of Westminster and the City of London quite separate entities).

Yet, despite the effects of the war with Napoleon, by 1803 the firm was able to offer to the Government the use of 400 horses, 50 wagons and 28 boats when he threatened to invade! But whilst the business presented an affluent face to the world by rapid expansion, (the barge fleet alone had increased from 10 in 1795 to 28 in 1803 and to over 50 by 1810), the inevitable spiral of borrowing to pay off debts was almost out of control.

Apparently other properties must have been mortgaged to the bankers Daintry & Ryle of Macclesfield, for by 1815 between them and the Kendal firm, Pickfords had accrued debts of £30,000 (well in excess of a £1/4 million today)!

Thomas, the agriculturalist, had died in 1811 and his two sons withdrew from the business in 1816. Matthew was in Marseilles by 1820 and continued living the life of a gentleman, frequenting Brighton etc. The debts eventually caught up with his brother, James, who spent sometime in a debtors' prison in Hertfordshire circa 1820, although he managed to lead a respectable life thereafter until his death in 1860.

The Pickford carriers continued with the sons of Matthew the elder. Thomas married a daughter of Edward Hawkins (a former banker of Macclesfield and a partner of Roe & Co. brass and copper manufacturers who had moved to Neath, in Glamorgan where the wedding took place in 1808). Thomas and his wife lived at Ashley Hall, then at Deanwater, yet always maintained the family 'cottage' King Sterndale Hall near Buxton. He and his brother Matthew sold half the business shares to new partners in 1817 allowing him to retain control of the Manchester part. Eventually he paid off all his creditors in 1835 and died in Cheltenham in 1846 when his Pickford & Co. interests were bought out.

Brother Matthew, who had taken control of the London end of the business in 1817 at the Castle Inn, withdrew in 1824 but he too managed to pay off his creditors.

Incredibly although the Pickford interests ended finally in 1846 and the firm has passed through many partnerships and reorganisations, yet still today the Pickford name has been retained and is as well known as ever – Pickford Removals Ltd.

Francis Beswick, like his neighbour Matthew Pickford, also presented an affluent face to the world. By the time his will was prepared in 1818 (he is probably the son or relative of the original owner of the Mansion House) the development of the site had been extensive. Apart from house (in which he lived) together with its close of land and outbuildings, there was also a silk factory, warehouse, a smaller house etc. in what was by then King Edward Street. He had also invested in a cottage and 6 parcels of land near the Turnpike Road from Macclesfield to Knutsford (Chester Rd.) and 4 parcels of land near Park Lane (bought 1795).

Beswick requested that his natural son, Joseph Hudson, by then resident with him, should take the surname 'Beswick' in addition to Hudson, within 6 months of his death. This Joseph did and in 1867 one of his granddaughters was still in possession of lands 'in or near' Park Lane, Oxford Rd., Chester Rd., and Beswick Street, and also held a share in the Macclesfield Arms Hotel, but by that time she was the wife of a John Froggatt.

The vast majority of Macclesfield residents who have been born and bred here are all too familiar with the Brocklehurst family's associations, both with the silk industry and the town, particularly in the 19th century and the first half of this century.

Nor do many need telling that Charles Roe built the first silk mill and that he and his family were dominant in Macclesfield affairs during the 18th century.

What is surprising is the failure to recognise the importance of the Pickford family to Macclesfield in the 17th century. They have probably been overlooked because of their nonassociation with silk, yet Macclesfield gained its reputation for beer brewing and as a consequence, its public houses through them. (Not too long ago it was said that every other building in Mill Street was a pub). Also I recall a significant little leather shop (cum shoe repairer) in Backwallgate which was certainly a survivor of the Pickford influence and their tanning trade. Another important legacy was the encouragement given to the dyeing industry, no doubt as a result of their involvement with the woollen trade.

At present the first trace of silk interests in the town is through the Rowe family (not to be confused with Charles Roe and his family – there is no connection between the two) and the Deane family of Manchester and Macclesfield, together with their London associations by 1640. However the silk industry must have been very small prior to the Civil War, otherwise one can be sure that the Pickford family would have become involved. But it is possible that James Pickford the elder, when taking his own goods to Derby and collecting the malt etc. could also have been carrying buttons and trimmings for onward despatch to London.

The button industry had certainly grown in importance by 1655 when Oliver Cromwell was Lord-Protector, for the Mayor, Aldermen and Burgesses stepped in to regulate the trade, to their own benefit of course! Yet even so it still depended very much on mohair, horse hair, ox hair and linen with very little silk thread required at this early period.

During the Interregnum Period (1649-60) there was a lack of enthusiasm on the part of Macclesfield burgesses to attend Corporation Meetings, but the Pickfords managed to maintain a modicum of normality. James the elder, who had already been Mayor three times (1626-27, 1634-35 and 1641-42), also took the post in 1652-53 whilst his son, James the younger (Mayor 1645-46), was again accepted for the year 1655-56.

The next generation saw the eventual heir Jonathan married and settled in Ashton-under-Lyne by 1669, but still retaining his interests in Macclesfield (his will of 1690 describes him as 'of Macclesfield')

The considerable Pickford holdings in the town were very useful when it came to marriage settlements, but apart from the land and buildings which were actually owned, other significant plots were leased.

There were three closes in the Dams under lease from the Cholmondeley family and ultimately subleased to Charles Roe, which consolidated his Chestergate estate. After his father's death, William Roe purchased this land, part of which today accommodates the western half of Roe Street.

The largest portion of land owned by the Pickfords was, of course, around the present day Pickford Street (see page 99) on which considerable development took place during the 18th century, part comprising Charles Roe's silk mill complex thanks to the various watercourses running through the area. If taken as a proportion of the Borough at that period the area must have represented about one third of the whole.

The Civil War period created much upheaval with some episodes shrouded in mystery. For instance the old crenellated house owned by the Earl of Derby on Mill Street seems to have come into possession of the Corporation at the time when the Derby lands were sequestrated and subsequently leased by the Pickfords and others.

Much litigation took place after the Restoration as the tangle of land ownership was slowly unravelled and the Pickfords did not escape. However they had worked hard to develop the area around 'Wellgate' (now Backwallgate) and owned two properties on the northeast part of Mill Street which had formerly been one large house on land belonging to the Savage family. Today this site would cover the corner plots of Mill Street/Backwallgate, just to the north of the 'Castle' site, and the development was very interesting.

By a deed of 1665 the Corporation leased to James Pickford the younger land in front of his dwellinghouse called the 'Corteyard' and amongst other items a stonewall extending from 'the gate unto the dyehouse'. This certainly seems to refer to the old Castle site.

Another significant holding was a malthouse and building 'with the Great Barne' standing near by. There is no doubt that this barn, referred to on a deed of 12th November 1711 as a 'Tithe Barn' on Barn Street (together with a house and premises) gave its name to Barn Street. It must have stood somewhere in the vicinity of the rear entrance to the Indoor Market now on Churchill Way. Originally Barn Street was that part of Churchill Way which extends south from Chestergate to a little beyond Castle Street, but then it curved to join Mill Street through what is now part of the premises of Marks & Spencers. Subsequently it was given the name of Derby Street (after the Earl of Derby) before part of its conversion to Churchill Way.

Different deeds indicate that the house and small backside close by 'the Great Barne' were

Edwardian Chestergate showing buidings on the far right where today Churchill Way cuts through. In the 17th century, round the corner to the left stood the 'Great Barne'. Photograph courtesy of A. Rowbotham.

Rear of the present Indoor Market on Churchill Way. Somewhere in this area stood the 'Great Barne'.

Another delightful photograph of Chestergate taken about the beginning of this century. The buildings to the right (behind the horses and carts) indicate the area in which the Gatehouse stood and to the rear was the land and buildings in possession of the Pickford family.

on the north side of Dog Lane which allowed the owner (or occupier) the facility of using the middingstead in Dog Lane. (Dog Lane was renamed Stanley Street, most of which was demolished 30 years ago for the Indoor Market development).

By a deed of 1712 this house and small backside, then in the ownership of John Pickford, Ashton-under-Lyne, were described as standing 'betwixt the Gatehouse and Great Barne'. So where was the Gatehouse?

A gatehouse attracts various historical interpretations; it could be a lodge or alternatively a house over an entrance to an enclosure or park. It could also refer to a substantially built apartment over a city or palace gate, so to discover mention of a gatehouse on a Macclesfield property deed is of great interest.

It need not have been a grandiose affair, after all John of Macclesfield's crenellated house had been elevated to the status of a palace, when in the ownership of the Dukes of Buckingham, and eventually a castle by the townsfolk of Macclesfield, but nevertheless the gatehouse appears to indicate an entrance to something.

The first obvious choice would have been to 'The Palace' which actually stood one block back from Mill St. (originally known as the King's Highway); the purchase of a plot of land in front of the house encouraged the creation of a courtyard later to be called 'the Placeyard Yard' and later still corrupted to 'Palaceyard', which presumably would have had an entrance of some form or other.

However taking into consideration the relationship of the Gatehouse to the 'Great Barne', the malthouse and (in November 1711 during the reign of Queen Anne) a dwellinghouse and other buildings 'lately erected', the Gatehouse was somewhere in the area of where the Royal Bank of Scotland now stands on the corner of Chestergate and Churchill Way.

Another deed some 2 months earlier (September 1711) refers to a different house already in existence on another part of the site, and all these properties were in possession of John Pickford, Ashton-under-Lyne.

The newly built house and buildings occupied part of the land close to where the Great Barne stood; the frontage measured 8yds (just over 7 metres) whilst the length backwards was considerable – 36yds (approx. 33 metres).

There is mention of a passage way at the eastern end of this house which separated it from the other house owned by Pickford, and rights were given to 'pass, go forth, drive and carry through' (presumably goods by cart) which suggests that the width was adequate for horse drawn vehicles. On this particular deed no mention is made of the Gatehouse, a probable indicator that it did not belong to Pickford and was therefore adjacent to his large plot of land.

From the details in the deeds we can deduce that the newly built house was to the west of the original one i.e. nearer to the present day Churchill Way. A deed of 1662 describes the original house, land and buildings etc. as on the north side of Dog Lane, and it is this original house together with its malthouse which stood between the 'Gatehouse' and the 'Great Barne' suggesting that the Gatehouse was in fact on or across Chestergate.

So the whole plot with its various buildings must have covered a large area somewhere in the vicinity of the rear entrance to the Indoor Market.

The corner plot of Mill St. and Backwallgate now occupied by two shops. On this site originally stood a large house known as a burgage, which became two dwellings in the ownership of the Pickfords. Their properties also extended down into Wallgate and part onto the Castle site.

Now we have an interesting synopsis. As mentioned in a previous article on page 62 there was a gate at the northern end of Jordangate, probably in the 'Pyrlewall' leading to Titherington.

Pickford deeds refer to 'Wellgate' or 'Wallgate' in the 17th century where a wall lead from the gate to the dyehouse, an obvious indication of a gateway situated somewhere in the lower part of what is today Backwallgate. Also we have the reference to the Gatehouse a few yards from where Barn St. (today part of Churchill Way) joined Chestergate.

Perhaps I might be forgiven for suggesting that the area of Newgate, just to the north of what is now the eastern end of Roe Street and adjacent to Mill Street, also had a gateway. The area appears to have been adopted fo residences in the Elizabethan period but it does seem possible that the 'Newgate' was a replacement for an older one which would have led into the parkland. This would then conveniently provide exits from the original mediaeval borough to the north, south, east and west.

Circumstantial evidence tends to indicate that the original parkland owned by the Crown covered a larger area than that in possession of the Cholmondeleys in 1788 before the great sale. Logically it would have reached Chester Road; a section of Barn Street; today's Roe Street; the southern end of Mill Street and Park (originally Parsonage) Green, so that not only the Newgate but also the Gatehouse in Chestergate would have led into the parkland from the small compacted borough.

(Unfortunately and sadly many early deeds have long since disappeared because of modern property development but there is still hope that given time many more may be tracked down).

A very interesting Pickford deed of 1711 refers to the leasing of a burgage property on the northeast side of Mill Street and standing on the north side of another street called 'Wellgate or bigger Wellgate'. As already mentioned, this property was originally owned by Earl Rivers whose family name was Savage and he also owned property on the south side of the Market Place in what had become known as the Root Market. This latter property was legally linked with the Savage Chapel on the south side of the Parish Church, suggesting that the whole block with its eastern and southern boundaries of today's Church Street and Backwallgate was originally part of the Savage parcel of land, therefore belonging to the Manor and Forest of Macclesfield and not the Borough: eventually plots were sold off allowing the borough to surreptitiously expand.

The burgage on Mill Street must have been quite large for it had been divided into two houses at some time. One house had a shop adjoining the entry and a brewhouse in the backside (? Castle Inn), yards, orchards, gardens etc. and a little stable with a chamber over it. There was also a warehouse with a chamber over the top and a great stable in 'little Wellgate or backwellgate'.

One of the lessees was legally bound to 'glaze & fix with glass as well as shop windows to the street all other such windows (of the house) . . . as are now stopt up'. The other lessee had to make 'a convenient light to staircase' (i.e. create a new window in the roof) but secure it from cold; make sure the kitchen was warm and make

'a new cow stall for horse (!) and a "Bowse" (bouse = cow stall) for a cow in the stable, together with 'a wood cover for the window there'.

These 17th and early 18th century deeds provide an important link with medieval Macclesfield, allowing us to appreciate just how large the original plots of land in the centre of town were.

Pickford Hall

When I began the Pickford family articles my hope was that eventual research would uncover the site of Pickford Hall but I did not expect to be rewarded quite so quickly. Thanks to the co-operation of the United Reformed Church Elders and their solicitor I can now confidently state that on a deed dated 3rd December 1783 the house 'commonly called Pickford Hall' together with dwelling-houses or cottages and other outbuilings including a large barn, had formerly occupied the Park Green site.

The land was part of a large plot known as Higher Eyes (formerly Heyes or Hayes i.e. areas enclosed by a hedge or fence in the medieval period) and, together with the adjoining strip of land called Lower Eyes (the area between Sunderland Street and the River Bollin), is often referred to in other property deeds for the area as 'Pickford Eyes'. This also included a small area referred to as the 'Eyes Brooke', this stream could have been what is now known as the Dams Brook, or the River Bollin.

The whole area of Pickford Eyes, which today stretches from Park Green to Waters Green and Wood Street to the River Bollin, has a complicated history. When in possession of the Pickford family in the 17th & 18th centuries leases were granted for industrial development, and often the lessees then sublet, but always with agreement from the appropriate Pickford Snr.

In this way, by the early 1740s, Charles Roe had begun a more intensive development of part of Higher Eyes nearest

View from Park Green. The central wall between Barclays Bank on the right and the United Reformed Church on the left marks the righthand side of a narrow path leading to the former large barn. The bulding in the centre at the rear is the Ebenezer Chapel of 1790 on Townley St.

to the present Wood Street. As his silk premises expanded he was allowed to demolish some old buildings on site including that of Pickford Hall 'near a certain place called Pickford Well' and replace them with new ones. The old Pickford tanyard at the rear of the house was converted into 'a garden or backside', but the small cottages with a barn at the eastern end of them remained.

A later plan clearly shows the position of the barn which was sold, together with the cottages, in 1783 to a butcher called Robert Greaves by Joseph Pickford. The barn stood between what is today the superb building of Barclays Bank on Park Green and the United Reformed Church, but was about 20ft back from the present front wall of the church and about 30ft in depth.

The plot of land behind the barn and cottages, which today is bounded by Townley Street; the Dams Brook; Pickford Street and Charlotte Street, was sold by Joseph Pickford on 26th March 1787 to John Ryle as trustee for a joiner Thomas Stubbs. Within 6 months the latter two had sold a portion of the land to trustees for the building of a 'Chapel Oratory or Place of Afsembly of a Congregation of Protestant Difsenters called Independants for Religious Worship'.

The building, in use by 1790, became known as Ebenezer Chapel. It continued to be used for religious services, with various changes of trustees and ministers, until in 1874 it was decided to purchase the plot of land on which the old Pickford Hall with its tanyard, cottages and barn had stood, and build a new church.

Two years later the present building, then known as Park Green Congregational Church, was completed, but the original Ebenezer Chapel still remains as part of the building which houses the Townley St. Sunday School.

By 1839 Pickford's barn had been converted into a dwellinghouse and there was a small roadway to the building 7yds in length (21ft) which is today represented by the low stone wall between the United Reformed Church and the bank. The first 21ft of this wall (almost 8 metres) indicates the righthand side of the narrow roadway which lead immediately to the entrance of the former Pickford barn.

Unfortunately the exact location of the house referred to as Pickford Hall is still somewhat elusive but appears to have been adjacent to the cottages on the side nearest to the Dams Brook.

Somewhere very close by was Pickford Bridge but not necessarily on what is now Pickford Street for that would only have led to the plot of land taken by John Ryle and Thomas Stubbs. As Charles Roe had extended across the brook and built premises on the site of the old Pickford Hall it seems more-than-likely that the bridge was nearer to Park Green than the present day Pickford Street.

The closes upstream through which the Dams Brook passed (i.e. from Henderson Street down into the Dams, then beneath the small roundabout at the southern end of Churchill Way and through to Park Green and the car park of the NatWest Bank) were all leased by Pickford from General Cholmondeley, so the whole area was therefore in possession of the Pickford family. The bridge across the brook was consequently known as Pickford Bridge, and the well close by as Pickford Well (possibly the one marked on the 1871 O.S. map half way along Pickford Street.

The plot of land behind the Ebenezer Chapel site bounded by Pickford Street and Charlotte Street was leased out by John Ryle and Thomas Stubbs the joiner, to a father and son both called

Rear of the United Reformed Church viewed from Pickford St. Pickford Hall originally stood somewhere in the vicinity of the building in the centre of the photo.

Samuel Hall. The Halls built a silk factory and dyehouse on the site.

By 1862 the dyehouse was in use as a turning shop and smithy and the silk factory and premises were occupied by a William Fisher.

Also on site was a dwellinghouse 'occupied as a beerhouse by James Bolshaw and known by the sign of the Blue Ball' (which had been licensed at least from the early 1850s), all these premises were adjacent to a 'building occupied as a school by the religious denomination named Calvinists', which is now, of course, the Townley St. Sunday School.

By 4th May 1899 the public house had changed its name from the Blue Ball to the Royal Oak in the care of landlord Arthur Hodson when it was transferred to Greenall Whitley & Co.

Until recently this property on the corner of Pickford St. and Charlotte St. was the Royal Oak public house formerly known as the Blue Ball beerhouse.

Macclesfield 'Castle'

There are two items referred to in the previous Pickford article which need clarification. Firstly there seems little doubt that the area referred to in the Earl of Derby deeds for 1634 as 'the placeyard' had become 'Palaceyard' on the 1871 O.S. map because of the early association of the Dukes of Buckingham with the mansion in the 15th century.

I am delighted to highlight the second item, because I now have positive proof from the John of Macclesfield cartulary, that the Water of E was the River Bollin. For a very long time everyone has been led to believe that the Dams Brook was 'the water called le E' and having no other evidence to contradict this assumption I also accepted the notion, however, having finally 'fought' my way through the cartulary I have now discovered the vital evidence clearly indicating the contrary.

(For convenience throughout the rest of this section I shall refer to John of Macclesfield as John of M. and his crenellated house as the Castle, and use the modern numbering of the deeds for reference: hopefully this should save confusion as the folio numbers refer to the cartulary in London which will be inaccessible to most people, but the modern numbers given by Bruell, the translator of the 'epic' work, are easy to find and available in a copy of the cartulary at the Macclesfield Public Library).

Deed no. 373 refers to a certain parcel (plot) of land lying quite close to 'the water called le E or Bolyne running down' on the east, and the date on which this piece of land was transferred to Katherine de Kyngeslegh, mother of John of Macclesfield's children, is 30th January 1415.

Deed no. 428 provides even better confirmation when referring to a plot of land 'called Huggehee with the houses standing thereon . . . lying between the water called le E running down besides it on the east and a stream running down from le Dom (Dams Brook) on the west'. The date of this transaction is 17th May 1414.

The unusual name 'Huggehee' appears in other deeds as 'Huggehe' (as in no. 400 where a ditch is to be made from the water in a line crosswise). From the position of the land a modern interpretation of this name could conveniently be 'Huge eye' because it appears to correspond with the later Pickford Eyes area.

Perhaps 'le E' could stand as an abbreviation for 'Eyes', although it does lend itself to another interesting alternative; in November 1996 I

wrote of the River Bollin as being named Jordan at an early date and the possibility that as Queen Eleanor of Castile had recently returned from the Holy Land when she visited Macclesfield and by tradition established the chapel (today St. Michael's Parish Church), it could have been at her insistence that the river was named Jordan. The river belonged to the Crown, firstly to her husband Edward (later King Edward I) and eventually to Edward of Woodstock, Prince of Wales otherwise known as 'The Black Prince, so could it have stood for a Royal Christian name?

Having established that the River Bollin was the Water of E, other deeds can be interpreted with greater confidence, but it is of interest to briefly relate to John of M. for he was the creator of one of the town's most important historical edifices, although at times it seems that both he and the Castle take on a somewhat elusive character.

His close association with the town appears to have started c.1391 when he was approximately 40 years of age and evidence exists to relate him to Thomas of Macclesfield, Queen Eleanor's bailiff although not as a direct descendant. John was a civil servant employed in the privy seal and sygnet offices who served Richard II until the king was murdered by the Duke of Lancaster in 1400. From then on life must have been extremely difficult until his own death in April 1422.

He needed to record his legal claim to his hard won properties (particularly the important Manor of Bosley) so that his five sons and daughter by Katherine, although apparently illegitimate, could inherit. It is thanks to this necessity that today we have much vital and fascinating information regarding late 14th and early 15th century Macclesfield.

A detailed study of deeds relating to the present 9 Church Street confirm the previous name of Churchwallgate and the original name of Wallgate for the street, so any John of M. deeds which mention Wallgate as on the west i.e. deed no. 472, are referring to plots of land,

An old postcard showing the view up medieval Wallgate before demolition of the remains of John of Macclesfield's mansion in 1933. From this window he would have been able to view his other acquisitions on either side of what is now Church Street This scene was adapted by B.W.A. Ltd for the silk picture of 1961. (see plan on pages 122-123).

The south facing slope beneath St. Michael's Parish Church which was occupied by tenements, gardens and orchards in the 14th & 15th centuries. The Dams Brook passed behind the buildings on the left to flow across Waters Green, and together with the water from the Town's Well, created an island somewhere near the Millstone public house (hidden by the bush in the centre foreground of the photograph).

usually with orchards etc., on the extremely desirable south facing slope with terraces below the church, and on the left hand side of Church Street when walking down to Waters Green.

Because of the apparent void in that area today it is difficult to imagine just how well adopted the area was; a glimpse at the 1871 O.S. map confirms this and suggests that Waters Green Terrace was previously 'Botfysslarder lane' as in deed no. 181 'a plot of land lying under the hill with a garden beside it and buildings standing on it' was situated between 'the lane called Botfysslarder and the lane which leads down from the market place towards the water'.

The Dams Brook originally ran behind what is now the Queen's Head Hotel on Waters Green and must have joined the Bollin somewhere on the north side of the railway station. It was only diverted back to what is now the Arighi Bianchi warehouse on Sunderland St. in 1769 to operate a water wheel at Pearson's Mill. Also we must remember the Town's Well existed somewhere at the bottom of today's Backwallgate, but where does the water flow now? A visit to the Borough Engineers Dept.

(whose staff I want to thank for all the help I have received over the years) confirmed that water flows down by the Millstone public house, turns sharp left and enters the Bollin through a sough close by the footbridge under the railway bridge, but it is difficult to plot its course which is concealed underground.

Deed 458 refers to an island under Alysondrebonke (Alexander's Bank) in 1344 which must have been near the site of the present day Millstone, and the lessees were given permission to use the wood growing on the island to protect it from the water.

A small bundle of miscellaneous deeds in the Cheshire Record Office indicate that in the early 14th century there were gardens 'lying at the end of Wallgate' – an interesting description. If the end of Wallgate (Church Street today) was the Market Place, then surely it would have read so? Other early deeds are quite specific when relating to property in the Market Place e.g. John of Macclesfield deed no. 289 which mentions his three shops with the gaol on the south (behind today's Chicken Spit shop) 'the cemetery of the church of Macclesfield' towards the east and 'the highway which leads to the cross in the market place on the west'. This highway is now Mill Street, if it was then called Wallgate why is it not named? The deed is of 1410 and the name Wallgate had been included in deeds for at least 100 years.

Accepting this, the end of Wallgate then becomes what is today Backwallgate, where two gardens passed from the Barker family to Richard Slegh in 1356. They are not described as burgages presumably because they were out of Borough limits at this time and encroachments onto Manor and Forest territory; they also appear to be smaller units than a burgage plot.

The Falybrom family held a large area of land somewhere in the vicinity of today's Queen Victoria Street and on 16th March 1383 (deed 70) transferred a garden in Wallgate next to the Slegh tenement to Nicholas de Upton. By deed 78 this garden was conveyed by Upton to John of M. on 20th September 1391. A little more than one year later, on 3rd November 1392 (deed 68) Slegh also conveyed his tenement to John of M.

The following week Thomas de Newton, who rented part of the Falybrom land 'close to the land which John de Macclesfeld holds . . . of William Slegh on the west' conveyed his interest in his plot to John de M. (deed 69) for 38 years.

John of M. whilst investing in property for himself at the same time was, in effect, acting as a banker for others and the most sensible security for loans was property. It would seem that Henry Dyot had borrowed money and redeemed the loan by conveying to John of M. all his properties on 1st. July 1393 (deed 61), amongst others this gave John two additional properties in the adjoining Godyaf lane.

John of M. therefore had acquired quite a large area of property in a relatively short time and in December agreed with Falybrom (deed 100) for 2 plots of land 'lying below the tenement of John de Macclesfeld in le Wallgate'. Tenement can mean several things such as freehold, but by the early 15th century was being used in the sense of a building or house to dwell in, a habitation, residence etc.

This infers that John had built a house on the site and is supported by the fact that three months earlier Queen Anne (first wife of Richard II and Lady of the Manor & Forest of Macc.) had pardoned him for taking 'without licence oaks from the forest of Macclesfeld to the value of £6 18 6d. which he had used for building houses in the town' between midsummer 1390 and 8th July 1393.

During 1394 John travelled to Ireland on Court business but by that time he had also acquired other properties, including two adjoining plots on the lower eastern side of what is now Church Street.

Apparently, for personal reasons, the Kyngesleghs made him a gift of a grange (barn), garden and land (deed 118) in August 1396 in Godyaf lane but his own speculations in the town ceased until September 1397 (deed 94) when he acquired properties from John le Boyle presumably in exchange for loans. This gave him further property in Wallgate (Church St.) and another plot 'with free entry and exit lying close to Godiaflone' (deed 90).

Nationally all was not well and perhaps anticipating trouble John of M. petitioned the king on 1st. July 1398 for permission to crenellate his house in stone and also for six further oak trees (for extensions to his buildings). One month later permission was given and the upgrading of the mansion began. In early 1400 King Richard was dead in Pontefract Castle, evidently murdered.

John's development of his site was restricted; he still did not own the front plot in front of his house (now the front part of Mothercare on Mill Street), he obviously could not extend into Wallgate and Upton's widow legally restrained him from encroaching on her property to the southeast. Therefore when the impressive stone porch was added to the front of his house it stood 80ft (24.6 metres) back from the present shop front and suggests that Godyaf Lane originally passed in front of it (i.e. almost parallel to the present Mill Street but one block back).

The earliest description of the 'Castle' is in 1460 and although only in brief mentions the hall (great hall) chambers and kitchen with a lead covered roof (a probable product of Derbyshire mining, although a lead mine had been discovered in the parish of Malpas some years earlier). Another brief account in the early 16th century mentions a croft of land on the backside, containing one acre and enclosed by a stonewall. (Recent building on the Aldi site uncovered a very early footing of large stones below the later stone wall, now demolished, in Boden Street. This was divulged by an experienced site supervisor who has recorded the position on a site plan for me. He insisted the stonework was of early date).

Rear view of porch remains looking towards Mill St. Using a plan of 1814 it was the eastern end of a slaughterhouse; without doubt an ideal enclosure for animals.

The remains of John of Macclesfield's porch before demolition in 1933; it faced west towards modern day Mill St. Including the buttresses at each of the four corners it was estimated to be 15ft square (c.4.5 ms.)

In January 1402 the vital plot fronting the highway was in the process of being sold when John of M. stepped in and with the help of trustees bought it (although eventually conveyed to him solely in 1407). One reason for this arrangement could have been his journey overseas. With the completion of the stone exterior Ellen Upton withdrew her encroachment order on 1st. September 1402 and actually conveyed to him a strip of land 27 standard feet long and 17 wide (deed 198) and referred to the stone residence he had recently built adjacent to her tenement.

One outcome could have been an altered access to Godiaflane – then made from the highway (Mill Street) down the side of the 'Castle' with a right turn. The newly acquired front plot was described in several preceding deeds (73-77) as in le Wallgate on the corner of 'Godyaflane' between a plot (then owned by John of M.) and the highway (now Mill St.). Deed 263 places it as west of John of M's tenement and north of another of his tenements, with the 'royal highway' on the west!

Any interests in Souterlane which came into John's possession in September 1397 have no relevance to his 'Castle' site. Souterlane appears to have been either the much narrower version of Queen Victoria Street which was eventually called Exchange Street East, or the lowest part of the present Backwallgate where the 'island' of buildings is sited.

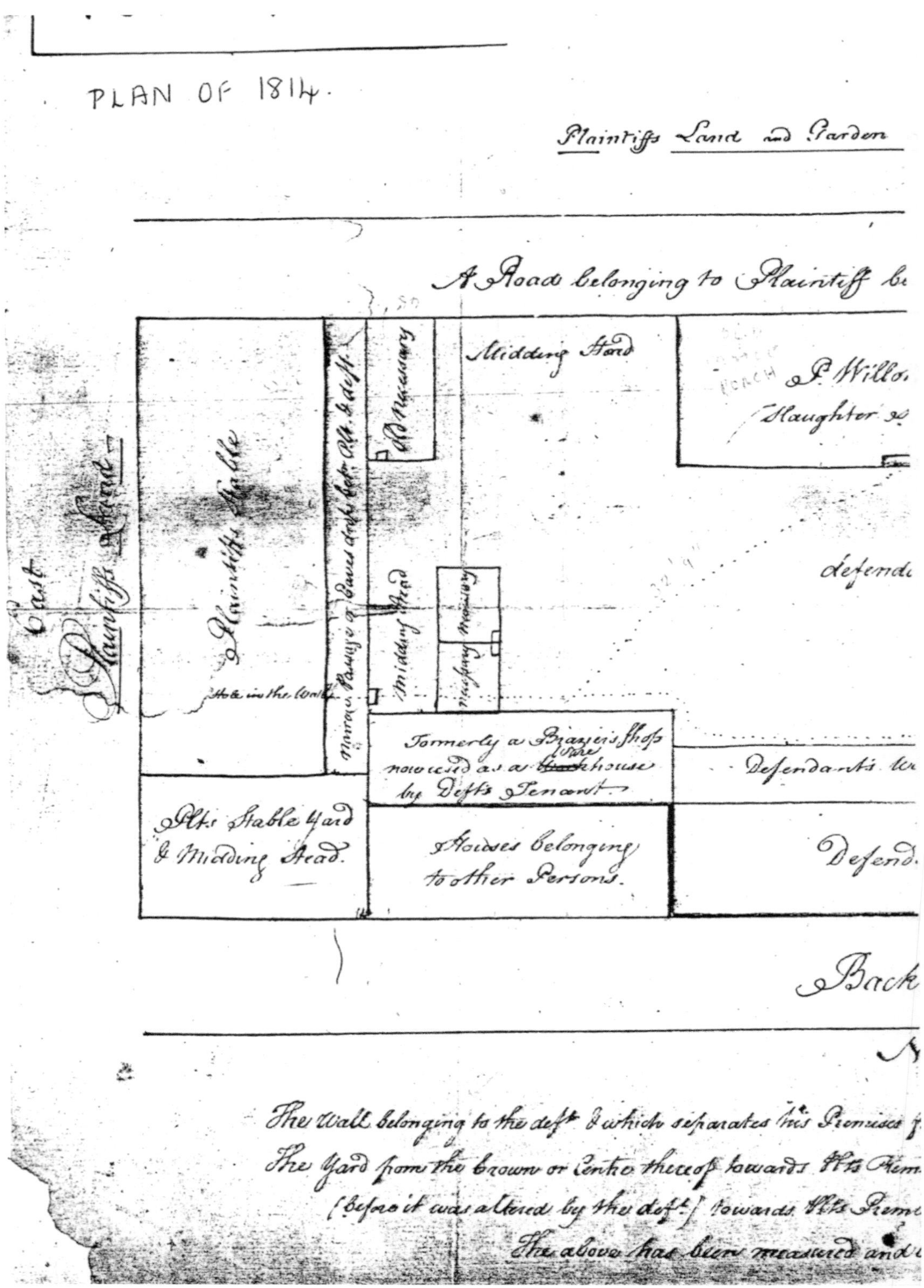

PLAN OF 1814.

Plaintiffs Land and Garden

A Road belonging to Plaintiff be

Midding Stead

P. Willo...

Slaughter &

Plaintiffs Stable

Narrow Passage of Eaves droft bey. Pltf. & deft.

D. Necessary

Midding Stead

Necessary Midding

defend...

St. & in the Centre

Formerly a Brazier's Shop now used as a brewhouse by Deft's Tenant

Defendant's Un...

Plts Stable Yard & Midding Stead.

Houses belonging to other Persons.

Defend.

Back

N...

The Wall belonging to the deft & which separates his Premises f...

The Yard from the Crown or Centre thereof towards Plts Prem...

(before it was altered by the deft) towards Plts Prem...

The above has been measured and...

Plan of 1814.

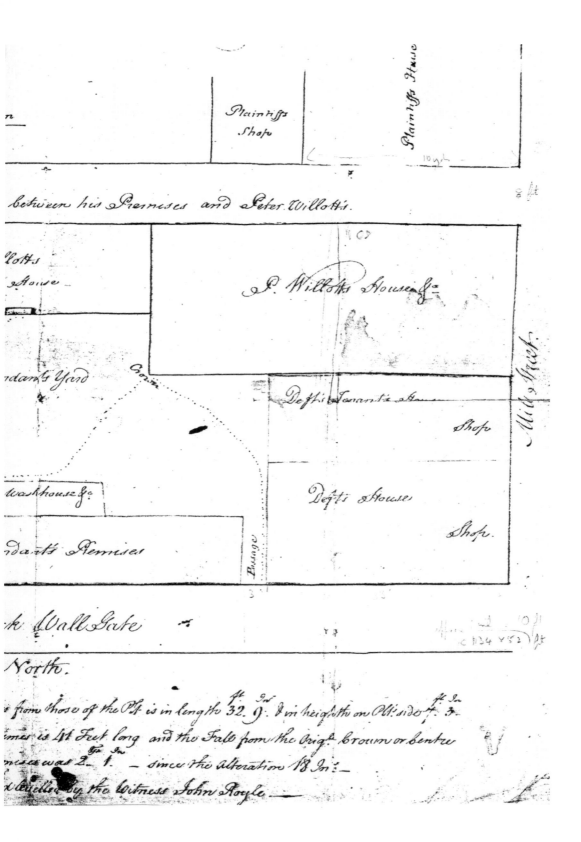

Plaintiffs
Shop

Plaintiffs House

10 y.

8 ft.

between his Premises and Peter Willotts.

lotts
House

P. Willotts House &c

Mill Street

ndants Yard

Defts Tenants House

Shop

Washhouse &c

Defts House

Shop.

dants Premises

Passage

Wall Gate

C 124 × 52

North.

from those of the Plt is in length 32 ft. 9 in. & in height on Plts side 7 ft. 3 in.

mises is 14 Feet long and the Fall from the Origl Crown or Centre

mises was 2 ft. 1 in. — since the Alteration 18 Ins. —

levelled by the Witness John Royle —

Christmas – medieval style

The Festive Season is once more upon us – a constant reminder of our links with the past. Although the present Christmas-tide, to a large degree, still carries the trappings of the Victorians, my research this year has uncovered some references to much earlier times.

In chasing up the Pickford family I inevitably became involved with Ashton-under-Lyne and the surrounding area, which seems to have been the 'gateway' between Yorkshire and Macclesfield in previous centuries particularly those of the mediaeval period. Along with people and trade came marriages between the offspring of merchants, officials, clerics, civil servants and the military etc. and also a diffusion of customs and ideas.

The Assheton family became Lords of the Manor of Ashton-under-Lyne at a very early date and a receipt for the rents of the manor in 1422 (the year in which John of Macclesfield died) describes the then Lord as 'John of Assheton Knt. the which came out of Normandy' (an obvious reference to an ancestor arriving with William the Conqueror). The tenants had to pay their rents twice yearly at the feasts of St. John the Baptist (Midsummer 26th June) and St. Martin (Martinmas 11th November).

The latter refers to Martin of Tours, one of the most popular saints of the Middle Ages who was especially renowned for his healing powers particularly amongst lepers. From the 15th century a goose became a popular emblem for him because its migration often coincides with the anniversary of his burial. The fine spell of weather which occurs about this period is known as St. Martin's summer and it was a tradition in England at that time to kill cattle for salting in preparation for the winter. It was also the usual interval between autumn and winter proper for the hiring of servants.

The normal rent payment dates for Macclesfield tenants were the feast of St. Barnabas (11th June) and All Saints (1st November) although certain tenants in Sutton did pay their rents on the same days as the Assheton

A Victorian engraving entitled 'A Michaelmas Vision' although depicting a Georgian parson selecting his goose; his Victorian counterpart would have also enjoyed his for Christmas dinner.

tenants at Midsummer and Martinmas.

In November 1396 John of Macclesfield acquired the title to the manor of Bosley from the dowager countess of Salisbury; this was one of the most extensive and valuable manors in Cheshire and even there the tenants rents were due Midsummer and Martinmas as in Sutton and Assheton.

Certain properties in Macclesfield had, what is known as, a quit-rent payable on them. This was paid either by a freeholder or copyholder (the latter a tenant of the manor) to release him from duties he might otherwise need to fulfil for the lord of the manor. As life styles changed this rent was really only an acknowledgement of an out-of-date concession and in later centuries a peppercorn was a common payment. Some John of Macclesfield deeds carry the payment of a rose at Midsummer (e.g. deed no. 70) as quit-rent, proving this property was on manor land. A very unusual quit-rent appears on one property (deed no. 66) but only for the three years 1366-68; it was a pair of white gloves at Michaelmas (29th September).

For each burgage property within the area of Macclesfield Borough an annual quit-rent of twelve pence in silver was paid to the Earl of Chester as lord of Macclesfield. This was due in three instalments; on the feast of St. Hilary (at that period 14th January), at Holy Trinity (which is the Sunday after Whitsunday and therefore a variable date) and Michaelmas (29th September). To our modern way of thinking this all sounds very confusing, yet our ancestors would have organised their lives around the Feast Days and would have easily remembered when the rents were payable.

In addition to rents paid, the Assheton tenants also gave their lord presents at 'Yule' (Christmas) and in return the lord of the manor fed 'all his said tenants and their wives, upon Yule-day, at the dinner. They shall send neither man nor woman in their name, except their son or daughter.'

The Yule Feast was synonymous with the Ale Feast and in Yorkshire and parts of Lancashire. It was the custom to burn a large log of wood on Christmans Eve, this was obviously referred to as the 'Yule log'. The family gathered around it 'to take a mess of creed wheat (the word creed = cree, which means to soften by boiling) which was boiled in milk and spiced, called furmenty'.

The stories handed down included supposed descriptions of the gatherings at Assheton Hall, said to have been typical of many other manor houses, especially in Lancashire. The lord and his family took their places in the gallery which ran along one side of the great hall, whilst the tenants feasted and made merry below. Pig tankards were used and horns

which 'bore the names of Saxons and Danes, whom the Normans had ousted out of their possessions'.

Music, of course, played its part in the form of an ancient fiddle and the stringed instrument called virginals. The songs traditionally recalled the deeds of Launcelot of the Lake, the giant slayer; Ranulph of Chester and his crusade; and Roger de Calverley's amorous feats! If anyone became 'unruly' their fingers were placed in a miniature version of stone stocks, about 18ins (46cms) long, which was in the custody of 'the king of misrule' and used as appropriate; just such a person was listed as 'Hobbe the King' at Assheton.

No doubt such customs spread into Cheshire, but one can imagine a more sophisticated banquet taking place in the great hall of John of Macclesfield's mansion, served from his kitchen close by (mentioned last month). The Court of Richard II was renowned for its cuisine and senoir civil servants, such as John, were well provided for.

Before taking leave of one of our most prominent townsmen until the New Year, it is appropriate to mention that Henry IV (as Earl of Chester) granted John of M. a 12 year lease of the herbage and pasture of the park together with the house in the park and 'le Ympeyard'. There seems little doubt that this house would have been where the parker or park keeper lived with the 'Hempeyard' at the rear and today the site is occupied by Harvest Printers Ltd. at the top of Park St.

Christmas scene: Harvest Printers Ltd. where a Christmas tree and lights always decorate the upper windows at this season of the year. This was the site of the ancient park keeper's house.

New Year – Georgian news items

Incredibly, not until the New Year of 1811, in the later stages of the Napoleonic Wars, did the people of Macclesfield and District at last have a chance of reading their own local newspaper. The first edition of the *Macclesfield Courier* was actually published on 2nd February, but even then there was little local news compared with that reported from London and overseas.

Until this significant event Macclesfield news of worthwhile interest or notices of sales etc. had been reported in *The Manchester Magazine* (and later the *Manchester Mercury*), *Drewry's Derby Mercury* or the Chester paper Adam's *Weekly Courant*, all with a surprisingly wide circulation. Three good examples are the following:

On Tuesday 21st August 1742 Samson Salt a Macclesfield grocer advertised in the *Manchester Magazine* in the hope that someone had 'a mind to take his Shop situate in the Mill Street in Macclesfield' and also purchase his stock; he was willing to allow 12 months credit providing security was given. (This is probably the man who sold two locks – charge one shilling, to the Churchwardens of the Parochial Chapel in 1738 but gained considerable notoriety in 1745 when sent as a spy to Stockport at the approach of Bonnie Prince Charlie's army. His subsequent capture by the rebels and forced march to Macclesfield and beyond, proved too much for him. Having managed to escape Samson was picked up by the King's forces near Stone, but rambling incoherently was released. He arrived home safely only to learn that the rebels were returning from Derby, at which point the poor man 'sunk down and died instantly'.)

Another somewhat unusual news item appeared on 12th August 1768, but this time in the *Liverpool General Advertizer*. There had been a 'great disturbance' in Macclesfield on the previous Sunday, when two brothers argued over a house left rent free to one of them by an aunt. The other swore he would level it to the ground and 'accordingly mounted the mansion, pulling down one of the chimneys, then began to unroof it, but he slipped off the building and was killed on the spot'. The deceased subject of this incident has yet to be tracked down!

On four successive weeks from 12th November to 3rd December 1773 *Drewry's Derby Mercury* carried details of a sale of lots of lead mining shares at Matlock Old Bath. Several levels were being driven for draining water out of the mines and were therefore, 'likely to turn out to great Advantage'. Amongst the several proprietors listed for further information, apart from those in Leek, Manchester and Chesterfield were Mr. Glover, Mr. Roe and Mr. Peter Wright of Macclesfield.

Even sales of mining shares to be held in Macclesfield were also advertised in the same newspaper. On 15th July 1768 notice was given that 'At the house of Mr. William Hilton, being the Sign of the Angel in Macclesfield, in the County of Chester, upon Tuesday the Ninth Day of August next between the Hours of Two and Five in the Afternoon . . . The following Shares of Mines of Copper and Lead, that is to say in ENGLAND' (10 listed in Derbyshire and 1 Staffordshire) and 'in WALES' (all 7 listed were in North Wales) were to be sold.

With the increased commercial concerns, and the rapidly growing population of Macclesfield in the second half of the 18th century, it is surprising that a local newspaper was not in existence, certainly by the 1780s. And whatever has been written on the subject previously there is now evidence to support the fact that a great many people could read at this period.

One of the first and most interesting of the local articles which appeared in the *Macclesfield Courier* on 23rd February 1811 was that concerning the Alderley Edge mines. Written by a Robert Bakewell of London, after his visit to the area during the summer of 1810, it had already appeared under the heading of 'A Cobalt Mine in Cheshire' in *The Monthly Magazine* of 1st February.

Although a scientist at heart Bakewell wrote with great poeticism, so delightful and typical of the Regency Period. His description of Alderley Edge and its panorama reads like one of today's holiday brochures: 'The whole plain of the county of Cheshire, with a part of Lancashire, stretching from the feet of the Derbyshire and Yorkshire hills to the sea: the pastures, woods and villages, the towns of Stockport and Manchester, the distant smoke of the city of

Above: The Derbyshire Caving Club at work: Wood Mine Alderley late 1980s.

Right: Pathway to Alderley Edge; an area inspiring myths and legends for centuries and hard-headed mining ventures, especially from the late 17th to early 20th centuries.

Chester, with the blue mountains of Wales on the horizon, form part of the features of the scene . . . The whole prospect comprises a scene of extensive and varied magnificence, which can scarcely be equalled in the kingdom'.

Even the scientific information was handled with great relish, 'In this place, in the space of a few acres, you may be presented with ores of most of the metals found in England; but placed in such situations, and presenting such appearances as are hardly to be seen elsewhere'. Having adequately described the ores in general to be found on The Edge, such as the blue and brown ore 'collected in nodules of various sizes, and imbedded along with pebbles in the sandrock, like currants in a pudding' he gave a brief but inadequate resumée of the work which had been undertaken by various mining partnerships. This, of course, included a reference to Roe & Co. of Macclesfield although not named as such, but was simply reported as copper ores taken to Macclesfield where, with calamine from Derbyshire, they were converted into brass.

After various pronouncements of scientific theory he eventually arrived at his chosen topic, the cobalt mine. 'The most remarkable production of the place is cobalt ore, which was very recently discovered here, existing in the red sand-stone'. (This mine, of recent date rediscovered by the Derbyshire Caving Club, is situated not far behind the Wizard Restaurant and close by the main car park.)

'The ores of cobalt, so valuable to the manufacturers of porcelain and paper, are very scarce in this island . . . The ore at Alderley is the black cobalt ochre of mineralogists. It is in the form of grains, of a bluish-black contour'. This discovery of cobalt attracted the attention of Josiah Wedgwood's nephew, who had ultimately taken charge of the Wedgwood potteries after his uncle's death in 1795, but who decided that the colour was too harsh for his wares.

Most of the cobalt, which had to be converted into smalt or zaffre for commercial use, was imported at great expense from Saxony. That from Alderley was packed in tubs and sent to Pontefract in Yorkshire for manufacture into smalt, but the production only lasted a few months.

Robert Roe's house

For many years a myth has persisted that Robert Roe's house was a property on Roe Street, now mostly in the occupation of Fearnley & Co. Solicitors, with the smaller portion on the eastern side converted into a separate dwelling-house; but this is not so.

For those readers unfamiliar with the Charles Roe story (he, of course, built the first silk mill in the town) Robert was one of his sons. The young man was destined to become a Church of England minister in the late 18th century but, persuaded by his cousin, Hester, he joined the new movement of 'Methodism' and therefore could not continue his studies for his church ministry at Oxford University. This had a devastating effect on Charles Roe, particularly after his considerable efforts to build Christ Church and obtain its Consecration.

There seems little doubt that Charles had hoped, at some future date, to see his son ordained minister of the church, but he died in May 1781 knowing this would be impossible. Robert's unfortunate stubbornness on many issues had seen him banished from his father's house, for his influence was affecting other family members and servants. It seemed most unlikely, therefore, that so soon after Charles Roe's death Robert's house would have been built on a plot of his father's land; two other factors initially also supported this contention.

The first was that Charles Roe did not prepare a will, so it took an appreciable length of time for William (the eldest son and resident of Liverpool) to be given administration of the estate and in the meantime Robert had already built his house.

Secondly, the strip of land on the south side of what is now Shaw Street and Roe Street (to Churchill Way) which contains the Dams Brook, appears to have been part of the parkland leased by Charles Roe from the Cholmondeley family in order to have water rights for his silk mill complex in the Park Green area. This area of land, which ran along the southern boundary of Charles Roe's Chestergate Estate, was subsequently purchased by William Roe, presumably at the time of the great sale of Cholmondeley parkland in 1788/89.

William then developed the area, naming Roe Street after his own family and Shaw Street after his wife, Hannah's family. The 1820 Land Tax Return for Macclesfield shows William as the owner of the properties and apart from a small portion which he kept for his own use, the other three were let. In fact Samuel Stone a doctor, appears to have occupied the Fearnley part (now 67 Roe Street), possible as a surgery, for his main residence was on Jordangate. If Robert Roe's house was not the property on Roe Street, then where was it? The answer is quite surprising.

In the first instance Hester, writing in her Journal (extracts from which were later published in a Methodist magazine) unwittingly led everyone astray. She wrote that after Charles Roe's death Robert decided to remain in Macclesfield and built himself 'a good house conveniently near the new church' (Christ Church). It was in a lovely situation with 'good air'; consequently this description together with the name of Roe appearing on the property deeds for the Roe Street property, led to the erroneous deduction.

Robert's new house was certainly built by the summer of 1782, for on 20th June Hester wrote that Robert, who was very ill by this time, had told her if he did not feel better soon then he would sell his house and leave Macclesfield. But this he never did and died in the property three months later.

The first clue to the site of the property is in a combined property deed in possession of Cheshire County Council. The deed dated 26th May 1813, relates to several properties in Macclesfield, amongst which was a dwelling-house previously used as two dwellings and known as Worth Hall on Chestergate. It also refers to a property built by Robert Roe (by then deceased) with permission from the owners, on part of the adjacent land called Worth Orchard; his house was also on Chestergate. Next to the Roe house two more houses had been built by 1813.

The next exciting find was a deed in possession of a member of the Macclesfield Family History Society which finally revealed the site of the Worth Hall Estate. Because of its relationship to a pool of water called Pinfold Lake

Not Robert Roe's house.

and the fact that the North Orchard of Worth Hall lay at the northwest corner of the field which abutted Chestergate, it has been possible to locate the site.

Several other deeds in the area show that the Charles Roe Estate extended, on the northern side, from what is now Charles Roe House on Chestergate to Catherine Street, then along Catherine Street to Pierce Street; west to what is now Great Queen Street and along Chester Road to at least Langford Street.

The part of the field on which Robert built his house was at the eastern end of Worth Orchard and divided from the North Orchard by a hedge. In other words it had to be on Chestergate between Catherine Street and Pinfold Street. The date on which he leased the land was 3rd. November 1781 with a Ground Rent of £7 13s. which today would be very near £1,000 per annum.

The descriptions from the various deeds indicate that by 1813, apart from Worth Hall and Robert Roe's house, two more dwelling-houses had been built. Modern alterations at ground floor level, particularly to accommodate shop fronts, can have a confusing effect, but a look at upper storeys can be very illuminating. The properties today which comprise the extreme southwestern block of Chestergate (i.e. nos. 106 - 116) relate to only three original Georgian properties and 106/8 was Robert Roe's house.

Worth Hall, modernised in the late 18th century, is now Chester's Restaurant and Robert's house was evidently designed to co-exist with Worth Hall, for the windows are identical in designed. With an increasing population creating a demand for houses, two more were subsequently built on the site (now 110-116) without the same care for detail, after all by then it was the time of the Napoleonic Wars.

Robert Roe's house on Chestergate (now 106/8).

Worth Hall on the right, modernised in the late 18th century.

Rev. David Simpson

Two hundred years ago Macclesfield said farewell to one of its most prominent, popular, and yet at times, controversial characters – David Simpson. He had arrived in the town during the summer of 1772 at the invitation of Charles Roe (the successful silk and copper industrialist) apparently through an association with a relative of Charles Roe's wife, Rachel Harriott. The reason for the visit was the vacancy of Assistant Curate at the Parochial Chapel of St. Michael's (now the Parish Church) and although Charles could not directly nominate Rev. Simpson, he could encourage the choice if desirable. He wanted to meet the young man and at the same time give the minister a chance to see Macclesfield and the Prime Curate, John Burscoe, with whom he would work closely. All went well and Rev. Burscoe together with the chapel wardens and several 'principal Inhabitants of the Town' nominated him for the vacancy.

The Bishop of Chester accepted the nomination and Rev. Burscoe agreed the sharing of the duties. Fate, however, was about to take a hand; five months later Burscoe had died leaving David Simpson in temporary charge of the Parochial Chapel.

It was a considerable responsibility for, together with the seven smaller townships i.e. Hurdsfield, Sutton etc., Macclesfield town could boast of a population of about 14,000 people within the chapelry jurisdiction. David Simpson grasped his opportunity and began with great zeal; too much for some congregation members, but he was newly married and his wife's uncle and John Wesley were great friends, hence the influence.

Born 12th October 1745 near Northallerton in the East Riding of Yorkshire, son of a farm bailiff, David Simpson

Miniature of David Simpson. Courtesy of the Macclesfield Museums Trust.

was only a few months older than Charles Roe's eldest son, William. Brilliant at mathematics he had received a Grammar School education before entering St. John's College, Cambridge in October 1765 at the rather late age of 20 years having rejected the idea of farming and now intent on ordination.

At that time great religious debates were taking place in the university and more liberal views expounded and inevitably Simpson was drawn into the controversies, a situation which would continue for the rest of his life; he was a Yorkshireman intent on speaking his mind, although a mathematical brain can often be at a disadvantage when dealing with human nature.

Ordained by the Bishop of London, his first curacy was in Essex where, being used to a farming community, he was happily accepted. Perhaps feeling in need of a challenge, after only one year he moved to the wealthier parish of Buckingham where almost at once there was resentment at his preachings, until the Bishop called him to account, delivered an admonition and concluded, 'If, Sir, you are determined to do your duty, as a clergyman aught to do, you must everywhere expect to meet with opposition'.

Now Macclesfield seemed to present a future for the Evangelical preacher, who firmly believed that a person's destiny is preordained and nothing will alter it. Finding himself acting as Prime Curate with the ability to fill St. Michael's every Sunday, as people flocked to hear him preach, perhaps he had every right to believe he would be given the Prime Curacy, especially as he had the support of so many, including the Mayor and Corporation.

The decision on his position was a joint affair between the Mayor and Bishop of Chester, but whereas in the past the Mayor had suggested a candidate acceptable to the Corporation and inhabitants, and the Bishop had agreed with the choice, on this occasion the Bishop overruled in the matter and insisted on having his own candidate ordained.

So great was the feeling of betrayal amongst

the Macclesfield populace that feelings ran high, especially when the new minister, Rev, Hewson, refused to co-operate with David Simpson, claiming most of the duties and fees for himself; the accusation being that Rev. Simpson was a Methodist.

Charles Roe, desperately trying to calm the situation, had offered as a compromise a piece of his land for an urgently needed burial ground, together with a small mortuary chapel, but now the Bishop's decision saw this indefatigable character leap into action, spurred on by his anger. After a further two years of 'enemy' intrigues he built his own church alongside the burial ground on his own land, and overcoming further complications, legalities (including as Act of Parliament) and a new Bishop, finally succeeded in obtaining consecration of the Church in 1779 with David Simpson as its first minister. There Simpson remained for the rest of his life, dying on 24th March 1799.

He had purchased early two plots in the graveyard, and although recent excavations by the Borough Council have erased all traces of his grave, it should lie immediately alongside and to the west of the carriage way leading from Great King Street, but very near the church and immediately in front of the railings which mark the original southern boundary between the graveyard and the church.

Wesley's initial connections with Christ Church are tenuous. He had attended St. Michael's on Easter Day 1774 with the Mayor and both curates Hewson and Simpson, and was therefore invited by Rev. Simpson to preach in the New Church (Christ Church) during his visit of 1777. Charles Roe, desperate that Methodism should not be associated with his church, evidently forbad Wesley to preach there and not until the spring of 1782 (a year after Roe's death) did he appear again in the church.

David Simpson worked hard during his ministry. He established a school where he taught early mornings, often by candlelight. He encouraged Sunday School and created a Society for women. He dispensed medicine free to the needy and in 1789 wrote an important discourse encouraging inoculation against smallpox, which was written to the four surgeons in the town (one being Samuel Stone mentioned in the freemasons article).

He vehemently opposed Sunday opening for shops (nothing is new) accusing the shopkeepers in his congregation of leaving behind children and servants to run their businesses for a few hours whilst they attended church.

His character is perhaps best seen through his own written words 'I love my family better than myself. I love my country better than my family, but I love mankind in general better than my country'.

The Simpson Memorial, Christ Church.

Margery Meadow

At last spring is in the air, so it seems an appropriate time to mention a piece of meadowland in Macclesfield which weaved its way through local history for at least 500 years.

The Christadelphian Hall, Pinfold St. behind which (to the right of the photo) there was a fountain which fed Pickford (Pinfold) lake or pool. The land at one time was part of the Roe estate.

One of the earliest mentions is in 1332 when it is referred to by the very interesting name of Margeriesmedewe (Marjory's Meadow), later to become known as the Margery Meadow. The earlier name is probably a good indication of its origin and is likely to have come about because of a marriage settlement.

Margery seems to have been a popular name amongst the wives of burgesses in 14th century Macclesfield, but at the early date of 1332 it most likely refers to the wife of Adam Byrom. She appears on another deed of 1323 concerning land leased to her husband by Edmund del Downes, and is shown as entitled to continue the leasing after her husband's death. Unfortunately this piece of land is not named but could be the plot subsequently to become known as Margeriesmedewe.

The family name was de Burun, one of whom had arrived as a knight in William the Conqueror's army. They became a prolific family, particularly in Nottinghamshire and Lancashire, but as the different branches spread out the name acquired various spellings e.g. Birom, Byram, Byron etc. and – yes – one of the eventual descendants was Lord Byron. Adam, the Macclesfield burgess was probably from the family closely associated with Manchester and Clayton Hall.

The famous Victorian historian, Earwaker, quotes Adam's name as appearing in a charter of 1302 (Edward I's reign) and also as mayor of Macclesfield 1357-58, although the Town Hall list shows John Biran as mayor 1357-58. However Earwaker does state that a John Byron was present at an Inquisition (i.e. enquiry) held in Macclesfield during 1294.

Land was an extremely important commodity in earlier centuries when every square inch was jealously guarded, fought over or the subject of endless litigations. It was used as collateral time after time when loans were needed. It is a fallacy to believe that people could exist solely on the profits from rents; just as today the vast majority of great landowners, and smaller ones, had business interests. The best security was to invest some of their profits in property, so that when the lean times came they could either borrow money against their holdings, or sell.

More often than not they borrowed, hoping things would get better, but if they were unable to pay the interest due, the moneylender was legally entitled to seizure of the property by taking the case to Court. If the value of the property was reckoned greater than the debt, then the money lender had to recompense the difference; at the same time he often took over tenants with the property.

Margery Meadow appears to have become just such a piece of investment, and the deed of 4th February 1332 describes it as 'close to the park of the lord king'. It was transferred by Richard Throstle to Roger de Cliff (Mayor 1339) together with one rood of land which lay to the north of the meadow and next to the highway on the north (today Chester Road).

Throstle had received a loan from de Cliff and until 'on a single day between sunrise and sunset' he could pay back the loan of 60 shillings and 16 pence 'without fraud', the land would remain with de Cliff.

There is now a hiatus in the records; however, the land evidently passed to the Kyngesleghs for, almost 80 years later, on 27th August 1410, Margery Meadow, together with the one rood of land, was given as a gift by Ellen de Kyngeslegh to her daughter, Katherine, the latter being the mother of John de Macclesfield's illegitimate children.

It is difficult to judge the size of the rood of land separating the meadow from the highway. Centuries ago when measures were supposedly standardised it was said to be 1/160th part of an acre, but even so acres varied from county to county, and as a Cheshire acre was more than double a statute acre, instead of equalling 30 and a quarter square yards, it should have been at least 64 square yards (almost 60 square metres). Nevertheless this represents a comparatively small area.

At present there is a further hiatus in the meadow's history until 1726 when, then in possession of the Pickford family, it was leased to Thomas Huxley together with a piece of land called the Long Close and an inn, the Queen's Head.

Almost another century passed until in 1813 it was included on a deed with the sale of part of Worth Orchard; purchased by a John Rushton from Sir Joseph Radcliffe (formerly Pickford). Its exact position is difficult to deduce, but circumstantial evidence strongly points to it being adjacent to Worth Orchard. The former lake or pool in the area was originally called Pickford Lake (misread as Pinfold!) and the Cawley map of 1838 shows a pool to the west of what is now the Christadelphian Hall on Pinfold Street.

Thanks to the kind co-operation of the Trustees of the Christadelphian Hall it has been possible to discover that their land was in fact purchased from Charles Roe's son, William, in 1823, but a plan of the site shown a fountain adjacent to the Hall's southwest boundary which must have fed the pool.

The most likely area for the meadow was immediately to the west of Worth Orchard; in fact the orchard was probably created out of the original meadow land. If the brick built shop no. 1a Chester Road (formerly 124 Chestergate) is disregarded, then I suspect that the row of four stone built cottages numbering 1-7 Chester Road (now occupied by an antiques business) are on the site of the rood of land, for a rough measurement shows them to be 5yds x 13yds i.e. 65 square yards.

The Queen's Head is at present elusive, but likely to be close by, and the Long Close is probably the Long Acre, again appearing early in the 14th century, but today represented by Long Acre Street running parallel to Chester Rd. but on its northern side. This does place the plots of land conveniently close together for Mr. Huxley's benefit.

The view towards Catherine St. from Christ Church. The buildings in the background on the right hand side now shield what was formerly Margery Meadow and Worth Hall orchard.

Barker's Croft

Having mentioned last month the financial arrangements regarding property in earlier centuries, it is difficult to imagine the incredible complications which had arisen by the end of the 18th century.

The Barker's Croft area of Mill Street until the late 18th century. Note the upper black and white facade of the Filigree & Firkin.

By the mid-century the Industrial Revolution was already well advanced (this is much earlier than has usually been recognised), and with a booming export trade inspiring everyone to claim their share, land and premises were leased out for industrial development.

The lessee often subleased, sometimes to several individuals who, on occasion, would subdivide yet again their portion of the premises and sublet to others, thus creating a pyramid effect.

If, in this chain of letting, a loan was obtained by one of the lessees to create or expand a business etc. the property deeds were used as the legal framework for the transactions. Therefore it is possible to have names appearing on property deeds of people who never actually owned, leased or occupied the premises, but were simply the moneylender (so a very clear head is needed from time to time in order to interpret the information).

One such area of development was Barker's Croft on the lower western side of Mill Street. In 1790 a piece of the croft was leased to Nathaniel Wright a 'Country gentleman' of 'Pointon' (Poynton) by the silk merchant, David Hall and a stone mason, Charles Broad. Wright then subleased the land, together with other properties, to Sir George Warren of Poynton.

Sir George in turn granted a lease of the parcel of land to a timber merchant of Macclesfield, John Morlidge who, in August 1797 subleased to a possible relative, William Morlidge, a joiner. (The exhaustive trail is now temporarily at an end!).

As I have previously mentioned, joiners at that period and particularly earlier were usually builders in disguise; two years later we find William Morlidge described as a victualler. Evidently, on part of the land, he had built for himself a public house, today represented by the Filigree & Firkin, previously known as the Bear's Head at 85 Mill Street.

Whilst William Morlidge remained as landlord, on 17th July 1799 he leased part of his adjacent land (i.e. still part of the original Barker's Croft) to a carpenter and a cordwainer (shoemaker), this suggests further proposed development of the site.

The eastern boundary was Mill Street but on the west was a coal yard; to the south remained a plot of Morlidge's land which he sublet and on the northern side were premises belonging to a George Nixon (as yet to be identified, but most likely on the south side of the present day Roe Street).

The exact extent of Barker's Croft, as it relates to the present day, is a little difficult to determine. It was originally part of the parkland and can be seen on the Cholmondeley survey map of about 1788 before the great sale. It is shown as 'Barker's Croft and barn'; leased to a Mr. Harper it covered just over 5 acres.

Its western boundary appears to have been at least that part of Mill Street between Roe Street and Samuel Street. On the south it apparently followed the present retaining wall which divides Duke Street from Samuel Street, but then continued at an oblique angle along what was later Elizabeth Street, but now virtually non-existent due to the creation of Churchill Way; it therefore included today's Duke Street car park.

In order to create the car park some streets of houses were demolished viz: Charles Street, Cotton Street (both of which ran parallel to Roe Street) and Silk Street (which virtually ran parallel to the longest part of Duke Street now bordering the car park).

Another property deed dated 25th June 1791 relates to a plot of land, again part of Barker's Croft, situated between what was to become Silk Street and Duke Street. By that date the owner was Charles Roe's son, William, still resident in Toxteth Park, West Derby, Liverpool, and it was leased to a stocking weaver by the name of John Parr. By 1818 there were dwelling houses built on the site.

After his father's death in 1781 William Roe began purchasing several plots of land and premises on the periphery of his late father's Chestergate estate, which seem to have then been leased out for development, as also were parts of the original estate. There are many late 18th and early 19th century deeds on which William's name appears, but it does not necessarily mean that those properties were originally owned or leased by Charles Roe.

One example is a plot containing two houses, a garden and a smithy on Chestergate which were investment property for The Macclesfield Free Grammar School (now The King's School) and which William bought from the Trustees for £400 in 1789. This was situated in the approximate area of what is now the entrance to the Grosvenor Centre from Chestergate (i.e. John Douglas, Gents. Outfitters, 28 Chestergate).

I suspect that about the same time William also bought the land close to the Christadelphian Hall featured last month, because, of course, his name is on the deeds for that area. (Since last month a reader from the lower end of Catherine Street has very kindly confirmed William Roe's name on his property deeds in 1794, but as this is an extracted deed the name of the previous owner is unknown).

I have not seen the property deeds relating to 28 Chestergate but if, as so often happened when several properties were sold off together from a large estate as an investment to a particular person, they were included on the same deed, this could have created the original idea that Worth Hall was situated on the John Douglas site whereas it was actually at the lower end of Chestergate.

The northern boundary of Barker's Croft is more difficult to deduce. Deeds relating to the hall on Roe Street, now occupied by The Salvation Army, reveal that this too was built on part of Barker's Croft. The land was in William Roe's possession when in 1815 he leased it to Robert Massey, a joiner, with the proviso that within a year he would build houses etc. on the plot. The tenants were to be supplied with water from the waterworks made by William, with rates the same as those charged by the Borough. (William also owned the adjacent land on which Fads is now situated on the corner of Churchill Way and Roe Street).

The northern boundary of the croft seems to have run in a straight line from Mill Street and parallel to the present Roe Street, but whether or not Wellington Street was part of the northern extremity, is at present not known.

The Salvation Army Hall on Roe Street built on what was part of Barker's Croft.

Hollinpriests' Mill Street properties

At the very end of the 17th century an interesting family called Hollinpriest appeared in Macclesfield. The name can be traced to the outskirts of Manchester, particularly in the 18th century when family members had biblical names such as Aaron, Abraham, Isaac and Enoch, suggesting they were probably Dissenters and possibly Quakers. The family was certainly not prolific, so it is interesting to find three brothers, Edward, Samuel and Robert settling in the town.

Edward was an Attorney who lived in Hurdsfield. He was married by licence to an Elizabeth Bancroft of Heaton Norris (parish of Manchester) although the wedding took place at Middleton-by-Oldham on 13th January 1698. The fact that he purchased a licence is usually a sign of prosperity at that period, because marriage licences were expensive. However, he did not live long, for his will was proved on 21st. January 1703 and his widow was left to bring up two young children, son John and daughter Isabella. That Edward was a man of means is aptly demonstrated by his long inventory.

Apart from his two brothers, Edward also had two sisters to whom he left money in his will; Eabothy (who was married and lived near Stockport) and Sarah who was single. The brothers, Samuel and Robert remained in Macclesfield, at least for some time and in the decade 1713 to 1723 five children were baptised at St. Michael's Parochial Chapel (now the Parish Church), two sons and a daughter for Samuel and two daughters for Robert.

What makes the family so intriguing is the fact that whilst they were here they occupied some of the Earl of Derby's most substantial properties, and this could be an indication of what persuaded them to come in the first place. Edward's marriage at Middleton near Oldham suggests some connection with the Pickford family, who were well established in that area by that period. Also one of the Derby properties involved was the old 'Castle' site (John of Macclesfield's crenellated house) which had previously been partially occupied by the Pickfords.

Although Edward had died by 1703 the rental list for the Earl's properties in the town, compiled in 1709, still records the Hurdsfield property as part of 'Mr. Hollinpriest's Estate'. This his widow would have been entitled to occupy for the remainder of the lease, but she had apparently obtained permission to sublet for the occupier is recorded as a Thomas Low.

The property comprised one house, one 'kitching' (at this period the kitchen often still remained separate from the house because of the fear of fire), one garden and 'ye daybrook pingle lying on ye back of ye house'. A pingle was a small enclosure of land, sometimes a paddock or close. Before the demolition of property adjacent to Victoria Park to accommodate the building of the Corporation flats, there was a Daybrook Street. It ran from Fence Ave. parallel to Commercial Road (but with Arbourhay Street in between) and almost reached Queen Street. Today the first half of it is covered by the part of Victoria Walk leading from Fence Ave. and suggests that the house could possibly have stood on the site where the Victoria Park Lodge was later built.

Details of the other two properties are simply annotated 'Mr. Hollinpriest' so it is not unreasonable to suppose that the two surviving brothers occupied one each. The description of the house in Wellmouth can be none other than what remained of John of Macclesfield's house. It was part brick, part stone and covered with

These properties represent No.3-15 Mill St. on the western side and close by the Market Place. In the late 17th century they were the site of a substantial property owned by the Earl of Derby.

The area often referred to as 'Wellmouth' in 17th century deeds. The trees on the lefthand side shield the site of the property occupied by 'Mr. Hollinpriest' circa 1709.

slate. The outside appearance was of 3 bays but the interior comprised 4 lower and 6 upper rooms. There was also a brewhouse, 2 bays of barning, an out 'Isle' (aisle – which was probably a covered passage way on the outside of the house, possibly created by pillars or arches), a court(yard), a garden and a meadow at the rear of the premises of just over an acre.

Also included was a large area of adjoining land which must have reached across Waters Green towards Hurdsfield. It totalled just over 12 acres, but these would be Cheshire acres, so today almost 26 statute acres. Just less then half of the land was known as 'The Goatfield'; another portion was 'The Comon Close' with a house and small barn.

The surprise is the third property which took time to locate, but thanks to a deed relating to 17 & 19 Stanley Street (now obliterated by the Indoor Market) the approximate size of this considerable property becomes apparent.

The Stanley Street properties adjoined Mr. Hollinpriest's lane but his house is listed as on Millne Street. The frontage was 17yds long (this seems to be Imperial measure i.e. just over 15 metres.) and contained 9 bays within which were 9 upper and 9 lower rooms. There was a cellar, a backside (probably yard) a barn, 3 gardens and two stables, the whole said to cover 40 roods; and last but by no means least, a twisting croft at the western end of the gardens 50yds, long and 5yds wide. Size is difficult to judge because a rood varied locally but should

have been 1/160 of an acre, so 40 should have been a quarter of a Cheshire acre i.e. more than half an acre today.

Judging roughly from the layout of today's buildings, and remembering access for horses and carriages and the Hollinpriest lane would have to be included, the whole complex must have covered most of the area now bounded by part of Mill Street; part of Castle Street, and the malls of the two Indoor Market entrances leading from these two streets, a large portion of which is occupied by Boots Chemist.

The brothers must have been involved in the textile trade and possibly silk, as a twisting croft was where the fine silk threads were stretched and twisted together. The length considered essential for the operation was 25yds, so the Hollinpriest croft was of double length. (Information on twisting crofts or sheds is available at the Silk Heritage Centre).

By 1743, the year for which the earliest Land Tax Return for Macclesfield survives, no one by the name of Hollinpriest appears on it. They seem to have disappeared as mysteriously as they came; perhaps they emigrated or moved to a more remote area. One suspects that maybe it had something to do with small town politics, for between 1716 and 1724 Macclesfield was without a Charter, which would have created a commercial 'free-for-all', but then a reconstituted Corporation saw everyone 'jostling' for power once more and it would be some time before the situation was resolved.

Coal Mining

For those residents newly arrived in Macclesfield it is difficult to imagine that there has ever been a thriving coal industry to the east of the town when looking at the lush rolling hills, yet around two hundred years ago it supported a vibrant and expanding industrial borough.

Briefly, the coal seams in the area (or what remains of them) geologically are part of a system of outcrops which runs from N.E. Manchester to almost the N. Staffordshire coalfield.

To date one of the earliest reference to coal mining locally is in 1382 when 'the sea coal in the Forest of Macclesfield was commited to the charge of a forester'. This does seem to be a particularly early reference but was quoted by Galloway in 1898 and, of course, could have been anywhere in the extensive forest area at that period. (Subsequent research has found an earlier date of 1353-54 in the Chamberlain's accounts for the leasing of coal rights in Macclesfield Forest).

Sea coal seems to be something of a misnomer for it actually refers to ordinary coal; several conjectures have been made as to its origin, one being that Londoners receiving their coal by ship from Northumberland gave it the name, and there is documentary evidence of mining in the North East of England from the early 15th century suggesting it had begun much earlier.

An Elizabethan lease of 28th February 1589 refers to an already working coal pit at 'Wourthe' (Worth near Poynton) and this does appear to be the area locally with the earliest development. However, in 1515 Hugh Manifold, who was the Coroner of Macclesfield, held a Crown lease which included 'miner lapid' called cayrage in the Forest of Macclesfield.

This sounds complicated but miner lapid simply means the mining of stones i.e. a stone quarry. Manifold, amongst other things, was also entitled to pannage, which meant he could charge individuals for allowing them to pasture their pigs in the forest; the word 'cayrage' therefore appears to refer to the charge Manifold could make in allowing others to quarry stones. It has been suggested that this is how Kerridge acquired its name and does seem to be a feasible explanation.

The word 'cayrage' appears in Welsh records, which in many ways is not surprising for Edward I took Derbyshire miners and several other artisans from this region into Wales to help build his castles. In 1352 (Edward III) there is a record of Alan de Macclesfield being a burgess of Beaumaris, Anglesey! The Welsh word 'caer' means a wall, city or castle (with which we associate stone), this could have been brought back by returning stonemasons, having become 'cayr' in Middle English, thus producing the word 'cayrage'.

But whatever the derivation the important thing is that when quarrying took place often other minerals were exposed, including coal, so what began life as a stone quarry could easily turn into a coalmine or lead/copper mine at a later stage, and Kerridge did become a coal mining area.

After the encouragement of mining in general by Edward I the next sovereign to actively become involved was Elizabeth I in the hope of becoming self-sufficient in the production of armaments etc. And whereas previously coal had been gathered mostly on the open cast system, the 16th century saw the creation of small coalmines hewn out in the shape of a bell. Elizabeth's great friend, Bess of Hardwick, was busy developing her coal pits around Bolsover in the latter part of the 16th century.

The Civil War period stifled industry, but after the Restoration in 1660 once again great encouragement came from the Crown, and the man made responsible for the practicalities was the audacious yet capable cousin of the king, Prince Rupert (said to be the greatest tennis player in the whole of England!). Sadly his premature death once more restricted progress, especially in the field of experimentation; also, although mining had always been a relatively expensive venture, it was becoming even more so as the mines went deeper, creating all sorts of problems.

Flooding was the worst one, coupled with the desirability to raise heavy baskets of ore or coal from greater depths, so before the advent of the steam engine (the inventor and blacksmith, Newcomen, had installed a steam engine to

Today the name is Gunco Lane which appears to have been part of Gunnecarre Meadowe originally.

The sentence is in a will of 1623 and reads 'And also one Close or parcell of land or meadowe lyinge in Sutton & Macclesfield aforesaid or in the one of them Called or known by the name of Gunnecarre meadowe . . .' The vicinity is in the area of Gunco Lane today so there is little doubt that Gunco is a corruption of Gunnecarre.

The word has an Elizabethan look to it, with the inclusion of the letters e, and we have an interesting meaning. Carr (formerly carre) signifies a bog, fen, wet boggy ground or a meadow recovered by drainage, and in the late 17th century was used to describe the sediment found in coal water.

Gunne is now an obsolete word, superceded by 'gun' or 'gin' (not in the bottle but a windlass and winch one!). It does not seem too far fetch, therefore, to assume that the area of land to the east of Gunco Lane was worked in some way with a gin in the 16th century. Could it have been an attempt to find coal? We know that on the ridge above (just behind the Beehive Public House on Black Road) there was a stone quarry, worked into this century. Also one of the main collieries on Macclesfield Common has left its mark a little further along Black Road and adjacent to Windmill Street (formerly Lunt Hill of the 17th century).

pump water out of a coalmine at Whitehaven as early as 1717) the preferred method was literally by using horse power in the form of a horse gin; this combined a windlass and winch (as illustrated). On occasion the winch could be operated by a team of men, not dissimilar to the operation of a capstan on board ship when raising the anchor etc.

Now we come to some interesting information, the documentary evidence was kindly supplied by Mr. J. Sutton who discovered the reference whilst carrying out family research.

A horse gin working at an 18th century colliery before the use of steam power.

Before the advent of steam powered engines in the late 18th century, which demanded larger and larger supplies of coal, Macclesfield was already consuming large quantities due mainly to the establishment of an important brass and copper industry on Macclesfield Common. The fact that the site had been chosen by Charles Roe in 1758 indicates that collieries in the area were already developing, and although there was no guarantee of how long supplies would last, initially the prospects must have looked good.

A little earlier, in 1752, Thomas Birtles of 'the Hill within Birtles' and involved in the silk industry, was in possession of what is now Charles Roe House on Chestergate, he also owned three farms in Hurdsfield, Rainow and Bollington.

These farms were leased to tenants and were very valuable properties because not only were there considerable quantities of timber growing on these estates, but also coal mines and stone quarries.

From 1759 Prestbury parish registers conveniently include occupations and it is evident from these that by that time there was a thriving coal industry, without doubt inspired by Charles Roe's growing copper and brass manufactory. Between the years 1760 to 1766 (i.e. the early years of the smelting development) the registers show colliers in Pott Shrigley, Hurdsfield, Rainow, Bollington, Adlington and Sutton, so one can well imagine the arduous journeys made on occasion to Prestbury Parish Church for weddings etc., in fact for anyone from these outlying areas, particularly in bad weather conditions and with the dreadful state of the lesser roads churned up by their coal carts, among other things.

The smelters (which stood with their eastern end almost reaching to where the Navigation Inn now stands on Black Road) required a reasonably good quality coal from which coke could be produced; this was an absolute necessity in order to achieve the high temperatures required in the copper smelting process.

Up to this period any coals found on Macclesfield Common would have been mostly used as house coals, but during 1758 Charles Roe apparently negotiated a coal lease on behalf of Roe & Co. with the Earl of Harrington. At that time the Common was still Crown land but the Earl had leased the area together with any mineral rights etc. from the King, so that he in turn could sublease in order to make a profit.

Coal mining now continued in a far more professional manner and the first colliery was called Greenaway, but unfortunately did not produce very high quality coals, however these could be mixed with those of better quality obtained from elsewhere for conversion into coke. Today Brookfield Lane off Black Road

View from Blakelow across Macclesfield Common to the town. On the extreme right is the old Hovis Mill and in the centre the spire of St. Paul's Church. The foreground represents the main old coalmining area of Macclesfield.

represents Coal Pit Lane of the Victorian Era, and this is possibly where Greenaway was developed.

By the 1780s the main colliery was Blakelow, described as about 'one mile fouth eaft from the town of Macclesfield' and as the name indicates, would be in the area of what is today Blakelow Rd.

At Blakelow the method used was to drive an adit or sough from the lower ground so that it cut into the coal seam as deeply as possible. (An adit is a horizontal or even uphill tunnel which you can walk or crawl into; a mine shaft is always vertical). This allowed the water to drain off and then the level could be worked as far as possible until 'interrupted by a fault'. The decision would then be taken to sink a shaft (called a pit) from the surface above, down to the level, to follow the new line of the seam.

Briefly the collier, using his pick, would cut out the coal from the floor first, but only about 4 inches in thickness (barely 10 centimetres) and then with wedges break it from the roof. The coal was cut out to about 3yds (2.7 metres) and then a pillar left to support the roof about 3/4 of a yard wide.

The collier lay on his side wearing a piece of leather on his knee called a 'cap', one on his thigh called a 'pilch' and another on his arm called an 'elbow patch' and wore only a pair of 'flannel drawers' (i.e. pants similar to pyjama trousers but made from a thick kind of woollen fabric).

The coal was put in a basket and dragged by the collier on a little sledge to the foot of the shaft; not an easy task as he slid along on his side, feet first, dragging the sledge behind him. The basket was then lifted to the surface by a horse gin or whimsey.

Often the roof required extra support and a lot of timber was used underground, particularly as the coal pillars were hewn away periodically to allow a better flow of fresh air to circulate. Also expensive machinery was used to draw off the water which continued to seep into the workings.

The seams at Blakelow were less then 2ft in places, but the main seam proved to be of good quality coal and therefore it was considered well worth the effort to extract it.

Long after Roe & Co. had given up their brass and copper business they still held interests in coalmines. Their mining continued over the Sutton boundary in 1792 when they seem to have taken over workings occupied by a John Clowes. Despite the fact that William Roe died in 1827 (his father Charles had died in 1781) the remaining partners of Charles. Roe & Co. continued their involvement until 1831 but then subleased.

In 1825 a report had been produced claiming that at that time 11 mines existed on Macclesfield Common. The Great Mine obviously the largest, although the seams were only 5ft thick, ran along the line of Buxton Rd., and above the Great Mine lay the Sweet Mine which provided good house coals, but none of the other seams in the Black Road area were more than 1 or 2ft in thickness. Whether these were owned or leased out by Roe & Co. is not known, but William Roe had been granted large areas of land under the Enclosure Award of 1804 which were around the Buxton Road, Blakelow and Tegg's Nose area, no doubt because of the coal mining interests in that part of the original Macclesfield Common.

Part of Macclesfield Canal near Black Rd. Before the cutting of the canal William Roe, by the Enclosure Act of 1804, was granted all the parcels of land along this section of Black Road presumably because of the coal interests in the area.

INDEX AND NOTES ON REFERENCES
ARE INCLUDED IN VOLUME II